Afro-Argentine Discourse

AFRO-ARGENTINE DISCOURSE

Another Dimension of the Black Diaspora

Marvin A. Lewis

University of Missouri Press
Columbia and London

Library of Congress Cataloging-in-Publication Data

Lewis, Marvin A.
    Afro-Argentine discourse : another dimension of the Black diaspora / Marvin A.
Lewis.
        p.   cm.
    Includes bibliographical references and index.
    ISBN 0-8262-1042-2 (cloth : alk. paper)
    1. Argentine literature—Black authors—History and criticism.   2. Argentine
literautre—Minority authors—History and criticism.   3. Argentine literature—
African influences—History and criticism.   4. Argentine literature—20th
century—History and criticism.   5. Argentine literature—19th century—
History and criticism.   I. Title
PQ7623.B57L4   1996
860.9'896082—dc20   95-40988
                                                                          CIP

Designer: Kristie Lee
Typesetter: BOOKCOMP
Printer and binder: Thomson-Shore, Inc.
Typefaces: Garamond Book and Gill Sans

For Judy, Monica, and Kevin—Latin Lovers

CONTENTS

ACKNOWLEDGMENTS

Thanks to the Archivo General and the Biblioteca Nacional of Argentina. Thanks to the Research Council of the University of Missouri–Columbia, to ACLS for a Grant-in-Aid and to the Fulbright Commission for a research grant. Thanks also to Vera Mitchell, University of Illinois–Urbana library, and Mary Harris, Missouri, for manuscript preparation and editorial assistance. A special thanks to Ricardo, Judy, Jesse, Ricky, and Patricia Ramos for their hospitality and support in Buenos Aires.

All translations from Spanish into English are my own.

Afro-Argentine Discourse

INTRODUCTION

The Afro-Argentine: Another Retrospective View

Background

The focus of this study is the contributions by authors of African descent to Argentine literature published during the late nineteenth and early twentieth centuries. This analysis takes as its critical point of departure the article by Josaphat B. Kubayanda regarding the creation of a minority discourse in Latin America. It is entitled "Minority Discourse and the African Collective: Some Examples from Latin American and Caribbean Literature," and defines critical parameters that are relevant to this study. This project is a combination of literary history and criticism, since it is necessary to ferret out, correct, and edit many of these texts before moving on to the analytical stage.

Minority Discourse and Afro-Argentine Literature

In an often-quoted article by Gilles Deleuze and Félix Guattari, "What Is a Minor Literature?" the authors explain: "A minor literature is not the literature of a minor language but the literature a minority makes in a major language. The three characteristics of minor literature are the deterritorialization of language, the connection of the individual and the political, the collective arrangement of utterance."[1] "Deterritorialization," we are informed, is the dissolution of a cultural space and is synonymous with "decodification." Deleuze and Guattari's definition of "minor" literature evolves from their study of Kafka and the

---

1. Gilles Deleuze and Félix Guattari, "What Is a Minor Literature?" 18.

1

German Jewish literature of Prague. They also allude to the fact that perhaps blacks can create a similar situation with language in the United States through the modification of English. Renato Rosaldo, however, questions the applicability of Deleuze and Guattari's concepts when he asserts that "American minority history should neither be ignored nor reshaped and assimilated to Eurocentric models of a minority literature."[2] The Chicano situation is closer to the language dilemma posed by Deleuze and Guattari than that of blacks in the United States or Afro-Hispanics who maintained no native languages.

Regarding the ideological dimension of a minor literature, the authors maintain that "because it exists in a narrow space, every individual matter is immediately plugged into the political." The assumption concerning the collective value of a minor literature is that "it is literature which produces an active solidarity—in spite of skepticism—and, if the writer lives on the margin, is set apart from his fragile community; this situation makes him all the more able to express another, potential community, to force the means for another consciousness and another sensibility."[3] The two latter categories outlined by Deleuze and Guattari are applicable directly to the Afro-Hispanic context.

Although Kafka, Germany, and Poland are at a physical distance from Spanish America, some literary concepts do transcend temporal and spatial boundaries. There are certain characteristics that exemplify literature written by those who consider themselves at the margins of society. Therefore, the constant effort to reinscribe, to recreate themselves as integral cultural components, is foremost in the discourse of so-called "minor literatures."

In "Toward a Theory of Minority Discourse: What Is to Be Done?" Abdul R. JanMohamed and David Lloyd observe:

> The theoretical project of minority discourse involves drawing out
> solidarities in the form of similarities between modes of repression
> and struggle that all minorities experience separately but experience
> precisely as minorities. "Becoming minor" is not a question of essence

2. Renato Rosaldo, "Politics, Patriarchs, and Laughter," in Abdul JanMohamed and David Lloyd, eds., *The Nature and Context of Minority Discourse*, 124.
   3. Deleuze and Guattari, "What Is a Minor Literature?" 16–17.

(as the stereotypes of minorities in dominant ideology would want us to believe) but a question of position: a subject position that in the final analysis can be defined only in "political" terms—that is, in terms of the effects of economic exploitation, political disenfranchisement, social manipulation, and ideological domination on the cultural formation of minority subjects and discourse.[4]

The articulation of the effects of economic, social, political, and ideological factors upon minority cultures as it relates to the subject position is, according to JanMohamed and Lloyd, "*the* central task of the theory of minority discourse." This is certainly the case with the Afro-Argentine minority.

In "Minority Discourse and the African Collective," Kubayanda delineates fundamental questions present in Afro-Hispanic minority discourse:

> When some of the problems of the real world of cultural contacts are translated into imaginative writing, as they are in the multiple texts in the Black Latin American literary tradition, we as readers are invited, as it were, to consider the protagonists or the poetic voices, themselves nearly always completely drained of their essence, as they pose and examine crucial group questions on genealogy, identity, and existential anguish. Who are *we?* What have *we* done? What has been done to *us?* What can *we* do? Where are *we* going? These are some of the major questions an Afro-Latin minority discourse addresses.[5]

These basic questions relating to genealogy, identity, and existence are posed by Afro-Argentine writers from the early pages of *El Proletario,* a nineteenth-century periodical, to the poetry of Gabino Ezeiza, a twentieth-century popular poet. This study seeks to provide some of the answers to questions raised regarding the presence of a coherent Afro-Argentine literary discourse.

Argentina is one nation that is generally overlooked in discussions of Afro-Hispanic literature. This is due in part to its present-day population,

4. JanMohamed and Lloyd, eds., *The Nature and Context of Minority Discourse,* 9.
5. Josaphat Bekunuru Kubayanda, "Minority Discourse and the African Collective: Some Examples from Latin American and Caribbean Literature," 116.

which does not contain many people of African descent, and to the tendency to downplay a significant portion of eighteenth- and nineteenth-century Argentine history, in which blacks were major factors. But it has been demonstrated, by Richard Jackson, Marvin Lewis, Caroll Young, and others, that in Uruguay, which is very similar to Argentina, a wealth of literature is waiting to be made available to students, investigators, and other interested individuals.

The most recent comprehensive assessment of the Afro-Argentine situation from a historical perspective is found in George Reid Andrews's book, *The Afro-Argentines of Buenos Aires: 1800–1900* (1980). Oscar Natale has written a very good evaluation of Afro-Argentine popular culture in *Buenos Aires, negros y tango* (Buenos Aires, blacks and tango, 1984). Neither book has the same focus as my project. Natale's study contains a discussion of the social experience of blacks in Argentina, as well as their role in the evolution of the tango. Andrews's research is based upon data gathered from fifteen weekly or biweekly publications by or about blacks that appeared in Argentina during the second half of the nineteenth century, roughly 1858–1900. Andrews relied most heavily upon *La Broma* (1878–1883), *La Juventud* (1876–1878), and *La Igualdad* (1873–1874). Since he was concerned with writing the social history of Afro-Argentines, the literary activities of blacks receive scant attention.

There have been articles and chapters written on the image of blacks in Argentine literature, but very little scholarship is devoted to the contributions in literature of this group. That is because much Afro-Argentine literature is found, not in books, but in periodicals published by blacks in the latter decades of the nineteenth century and the early twentieth century. Horacio Mendizábal, the romantic poet, is an exception, having published two volumes, and the *payadores,* or popular poets, Ezeiza, Luis García Morel, and Higinio Cazón, managed to have their works printed and distributed, primarily in pamphlet form. But it is in the pages of the now missing *Eco Artístico, La Broma, La Juventud,* and other periodicals that Afro-Argentines left their legacy.

This introduction to my study is a survey of relevant historical, sociological, and anthropological literature assessing the plight of people of African descent in Argentina. The introduction also discusses the importance of the black press and Afro-Argentine mutual aid societies in the transition from slavery to freedom, and in the advancement of their community during the nineteenth century.

Chapter 1, "The Romantic Mode in Afro-Argentine Letters," is based on my readings and interpretations of periodicals and archival documents. The chapter situates black writers within national literary trends and analyzes the works of Mateo Elejalde and Mendizábal. Their contributions are analyzed as products of the Argentine romantic movement and also as writings that reflect an Afro-Argentine ideology regarding ethnicity and class.

"Casildo G. Thompson and the Failure of *Negritud,*" chapter 2, scrutinizes the writings of Thompson and other artists who produced Afrocentric works. This chapter seeks to explain the paucity of committed Afro-Argentine writers in a society that was bent upon their extinction.

Chapter 3, "The *Criollista* Spirit or the Black Writer as *Payador,*" uses as a critical basis Adolfo Prieto's landmark study, *El discurso criollista en la formación de la Argentina moderna* (Creole discourse in the formation of modern Argentina, 1988), for an examination of the concept of *criollismo,* indigenousness, from a black perspective. The poetry of the poets/artists/performers Ezeiza, Cazón, and Morel is examined as manifestations of "native" cultural expression in Argentina.

"Cry for Afro-Argentines," the concluding chapter, is an assessment of Afro-Argentine literature over the one-hundred-year period covered in this study. It draws analogies between the demise of the black population in Argentina, its literary production, and its inability to sustain an effective minority discourse.

Afro-Argentine Literature and the Postcolonial Model

Writing within the literary constraints of romanticism and Creolism did not allow Afro-Argentine authors to break completely with national literary traditions. There was, however, the attempt to create a black "I" (subject) for the first time in Argentine literary history. Therefore, in regard to theory and critical methodology, it is necessary to maintain a balance between Eurocentric and Afrocentric perspectives. A strictly romantic/creole reading of these texts would only reinforce hegemonic theory without answering the basic question of what is *black* about Afro-Argentine discourse.

Of the theoretical models currently in vogue, the postcolonial seems most appropriate for this study, given the historical experience of blacks in Argentina. Postcolonial discourse embraces direct challenge of colonial rule, questions the concept of "otherness," and examines the nature of power, knowledge, and resistance.[6] Minority versus majority poetics is also a critical issue addressed in this study.

In a chapter entitled "Pluralizing Poetics" in his recent study, *Cultural Criticism, Literary Theory, Poststructuralism* (1992), Vincent B. Leitch writes

> Contemporary theories of literature relating to ethnic enclaves, oppressed groups, and colonized peoples call into question traditional claims for a single universal poetics applicable to all humanity. From this perspective the capacious poetics outlined by Frye appears as a Christianized Eurocentric model that bears little, if any, direct relevance to numerous literatures. There is not one but a plurality of poetics.[7]

Leitch's comments are appropriate in this era of theory-driven criticism where the tendency is to find a theoretical model and make a work fit regardless of its origin or intention. In the United States, Eurocentric models remain in vogue as representative of the universal, although there have been some recent calls for reason.

In *The Empire Writes Back: Theory and Practice of Post-Colonial Literature* (1989) Ashcroft, Griffiths, and Tiffin comment: "Thus the long-term importance of the postmodernist and poststructuralist impacts in America may well be in allowing the Americans to recapture and appropriate their own writing from a false history of explication."[8] This will never happen among U.S. Latin Americanists so long as the academic power structure seeks its intellectual impetus from trickle-down European theories that may or may not be relevant to the Americas. An educated person in a university should, of course, be literate in the latest developments in his or her field but, at the same time, display an

6. Current tendencies in postcolonial studies are addressed by Liz McMillen in "Post-Colonial Studies Plumb the Experience of Living Under, and After, Imperialism," A6–9.

7. Vincent B. Leitch, *Cultural Criticism, Literary Theory, Poststructuralism*, 83.

8. Bill Ashcroft, Gareth Griffiths, and Helen Tiffin, *The Empire Writes Back: Theory and Practice of Post-Colonial Literature*, 163.

awareness of the strengths and limitations of a given theory or critical methodology.

"Postcolonial" as defined by the authors of *The Empire Writes Back* encompasses "all the culture affected by the imperial process from the moment of colonization to the present day," because of the "continuity of preoccupations throughout the historical process initiated by European aggression." This broad conception embraces Afro-Hispanic literature, a minority discourse within the postcolonial paradigm. Several critical models are discussed by the authors of *The Empire Writes Back,* including the Black Writing Model, which "proceeds from the idea of race as a major feature of economic and political discrimination and draws together writers in the African diaspora whatever their nationality." There is also a discussion of African literary theories whereby negritude is considered "the earliest attempt to create a consistent theory of modern African writing." Finally, the elaboration of Caribbean theories include "Edward Brathwaite and Creolization," "Denis Williams and Catalysis," and "Wilson Harris and the Syncretic Vision." Of these three critical models, the Caribbean seems to offer more possibilities for Afro-Hispanic literature because it conceptualizes ancestry, the transformation of African culture in the American, as well as cultural syncretism. In Argentina specifically, the black experience reflects many themes attributable to postcolonial discourse, but African-based theories associated with ethnicity, negritude, creolization, and syncretism did not materialize. Afro-Argentine writers did, however, engage in a critical dialogue with the society that seemed determined to reject them.

Leitch offers some more remarks that are relevant to this discussion: "There is no ontology of literature per se; there are literature functions in relation to particular regimes and programs. Racist, patriarchal, and colonial regimes characteristically denigrate, exclude, or overlook 'minority literatures' produced by people of color, women, and 'natives,' all of whom must struggle against the effects of domination. The poetics of minorities emerge from heterogeneous, conflictual regimes, divided, oppressed subjects, and hybrid language traditions and cultural intertexts."[9] Minority literatures are not just majority literatures of a different color or gender. In Spanish America in general, and Argentina

---

9. Leitch, *Cultural Criticism, Literary Theory, Poststructuralism,* 84.

in particular, black literature is the product of "racist, patriarchal, and colonial regimes" that relegated this production to the margins of the Estuario de la Plata. The history of Afro-Argentine discourse is one of the struggles against the effects of domination.

Applying any type of "post" theory to Spanish America is problematic since in the majority of cases, we are talking about societies that are "pre" in many regards. Therefore, categories such as postmodernism and postcolonialism should be used with discretion. I do find, however, that the authors of *The Empire Writes Back,* who refer to the former British Empire, offer some useful ideas that are applicable to the situation of their Spanish counterparts. The term "postcolonial" is used by them to "cover all the culture affected by the imperial process from the moment of colonization to the present day. This is because there is a continuity of preoccupations throughout the historical process initiated by European imperial aggression."

Postcolonial theory has, of course, its detractors. In *Black Women, Writing and Identity: Migrations of the Subject* (1994), Carole Boyce Davies states: "Post-coloniality in this context, has become the center announcing its own political agenda without reference to indigenous self-articulations. For post-coloniality is a theoretical production of the Western academy (even though by some non-Western scholars) within which writers and teacher critics are asked to locate their works."[10] The implicit contradiction here is that feminist theory, which undergirds Boyce Davies's study, is also "a theoretical production of the Western academy," not to mention the "political agenda" of this particular critic and most others.

Afro-Argentines suffered the double bind of being slaves legally until 1853 and second-class citizens until the present, that is, victims of a dual process of colonization. Most of their writings were produced by "natives" or "outcasts" during what Ashcroft, Griffiths, and Tiffin call the second stage of the postcolonial era. Basic themes include the celebration of the struggle toward independence in community and individual, the dominating influence of a foreign culture, the recur-

10. Carole Boyce Davies, *Black Women, Writing and Identity: Migrations of the Subject,* 82.

rent structural pattern of exile, the tendency toward subversion, and others.

The applicability of universal theoretical models to minority litera- tures is one of the basic questions posed by the authors of *The Empire Writes Back,* whose attitudes parallel those of Leitch. They argue

> The idea of "post-colonial literary theory" emerges from the inability of European theory to deal adequately with the complexities and varied cultural provenance of post-colonial writing. European theo- ries themselves emerge from particular cultural traditions which are hidden by false notions of the "universal." Theories of style and genre, assumptions about the universal features of language, epistemologies and value systems are all radically questioned by the practices of post- colonial writing.[11]

It is necessary, therefore, to maintain a balance between majority and minority perspectives when analyzing Afro-Argentine literature. True, the written expression is articulated from the point of view of the oppressed, but it is written in the dominant language.

While one seeks to find the proper manner in which to evaluate Afro-Argentine literature, one has to avoid the fallacy of privileging the "Afro" over the "Argentine" or vice versa. Black journalists, writers, and politicians were products of their times as their contributions attest. Subsequently, *Romanticismo* and *Criollismo,* as literary movements, provide the background for the majority of Afro-Argentine writers under scrutiny here.

The Disappearance

The role of Argentines of African descent in the development of Argentina has been documented by a small number of historians, so- ciologists, and anthropologists. The significance or insignificance of their contributions has been debated, but only recently has serious attention been given to what Afro-Argentines have said and have been saying about themselves and their contributions. It is interesting that

11. Ashcroft, Griffiths, and Tiffin, *The Empire Writes Back,* 5.

they seem less militant, anxious, and concerned now, when they are on the brink of extinction as an ethnic group, than they were at the turn of the century, when they demanded respect, equality, and justice under the law.

Although bits and pieces of the Afro-Argentine puzzle have appeared for years, the scholar who did a masterful job of writing them back into Argentine history is George Reid Andrews: his *The Afro-Argentines of Buenos Aires* is a cultural history of depth and sensitivity, based upon meticulous archival research. In 1980, too, *Todos es historia,* the Argentine journal, dedicated a special number to "Our Blacks" that, more than anything else, demonstrated the need for more serious research on Afro-Argentines.

"[T]he colored people of Buenos Aires constitute a disperse group, in extinction, which does not constitute a community," asserts Máximo Simpson in an article published in 1967.[12] The people interviewed in his article express their discontent with the racist nature of Argentine society. Two other articles in which Afro-Argentines appear to be resigned to disappearing are also worthy of mention here. They are "Buenos Aires de Ébano," which appeared anonymously in the *Revista Clarín* in 1971, and the often-cited "Argentina: Land of the Vanishing Black," by Era Thompson, published in *Ebony* in 1973. The former article, by an Argentine reporter, and the latter, by a U.S. black, are similar in that they give testimony to the decline of an ethnic culture. Through the eyes and voices of black witnesses, the reader is presented with an insider's view of the culmination of a miscegenation/ethnocidal process that began more than a century ago.

There seems to be a sigh of relief by Argentine blacks, now that they are no longer perceived as the perpetual Other, society's pariah. But how does one explain the situation of a people who apparently will pass from history without leaving a meaningful trace, except in a few instances, from slavery to heroism to nothingness? In the case of Argentine blacks, in this century there seems to have been a lack of concern for their own history and collective identity in relation

12. Máximo Simpson, "Porteños de color," 78.

to their country. In contrast to Uruguay and Peru, for example, no twentieth-century Afro-Argentine cultural voices of national or international stature emerged to decry the plight of blacks.

In the *Revista Clarín* survey, a typical mulatto response to the question of the black social status in Argentina is offered by Jorge Boot: "Personally I have never had difficulties because of my color." Alicia País maintains, "On a personal level, my problems are the same as those that afflict any Argentine, it's related to the situation of the country." From Enrique Nadal, a black father whose mulatto son has been refused admittance to a kindergarten because of the color of his skin, the reaction is, "Basically it was a problem of social image. Because the school was upper middle class, the director did not want to admit a mulatto child fearing that it would raise doubts about the character of the institution." Nadal, at the time, is resigned to the inferiority assigned to his son and himself based on skin color. The final observation of Hector Obella, a teacher, sums up the attitudes of those interviewed and perhaps the ultimate plight of Afro-Argentines: "In our country we are too few to constitute a problem." Any attempt to unearth the "Afro" dimension of this population is often met with the response, "we are Argentines," period.

The 1970s saw an intensification of the never-ending debate regarding the reasons for the disappearance of blacks from Argentine society. Blacks, during several decades of the nineteenth century, were more numerous than whites in Buenos Aires. Wars, miscegenation, European immigration, disease, and a strong dose of racism seem to be the most frequent reasons given for the lack of a significant visible black presence in the present Argentine ethnic matrix. In this regard, Andrés Avellaneda makes a relevant observation to nineteenth-century Argentine historical reality:

> In spite of decrees and dispositions, economic reality and racial prejudices rooted in the soul of decent people served to perpetuate slavery for many years. Only war would end it. Filling in the holes that the apathy of many white citizens of the young country left, in the Army of the Andes, in the war against the Indian, in the swamps of Paraguay. The last survivors came out of the Buenos Aires

slums to give of themselves during the yellow fever epidemic in 1871.[13]

On this occasion, Avellaneda summarized what is generally known but not fully acknowledged by Argentine historians regarding the hypocrisy toward extermination of blacks in Argentina. That is, slavery was legally abolished in name only and many blacks saw service with the forces of liberation from Spanish rule as their only option for freedom. Blacks also served in disproportionate numbers in other national conflicts, and the yellow fever epidemic of 1871 was devastating to the black population.

The relationship between nineteenth-century Argentine immigration policy and blacks was also given serious treatment during this period of self-assessment in the 1970s. In his discussion of "Immigration as Part of a Plan to Transform Argentine Society," Gino Germani writes

> The primary and explicit objective of the immigration was not only to populate the desert, finding inhabitants for an immense territory which to a large extent remained uninhabited or only contained a low density, but, and above all, to *modify substantially the composition of the population;* and the basic objective highlighted the other aspects of the plan: education and the expansion and modernization of the economy.[14]

Afro-Argentines would be the losers in this equation, since, following Germani's line of thought, "It was necessary to Europeanize the Argentine population, produce a regeneration of races." According to Domingo Faustino Sarmiento, "no less necessary was to physically bring Europe to America (J. B. Alberdi), if a radical transformation of society and men were desired." In other words, there was an official, concerted effort to eliminate the blacks from Argentine society.

Other factors often referred to in the disappearance of blacks in Argentina are low birth rates and high infant mortality rates. According

---

13. Andrés Avellaneda, "Calendario-Mayo de 1812: Prohibe la junta el ingreso de esclavos," 8.
14. Gino Germani, *Política y sociedad en una época de transición,* 240.

to Marta Goldberg, warning signals regarding the extinction of Afro-Argentines were apparent as early as 1837. She writes: "The results we have obtained about birthrate, infant mortality and general mortality in 1837 demonstrate that the situation with regard to previous years remain unchanged. All of these rates are very high for both groups, but comparatively, much worse for the colored population, whose vegetative growth is nil or negative."[15] Given the unstable situation of the black family during slavery, it is not surprising that birth rates were low and infant mortality high.

Miscegenation is another reason given for the disappearance of Afro-Argentines. In her study *The Slave Trade in the River Plate Region in the 17th Century*, Elena F. S. de Studer writes: "But the greatest influence that the servile class had in Spanish American society came from the mixture of races. From the racial point of view, the black contributed to forming the most diverse types of varieties with Europeans and Indians."[16]

Regarding the question of miscegenation, Mariano G. Bosch writes: "Another important factor contributed to the disappearance of the black race, before so numerous: the Italian. The latter had perhaps an atavistic preference for black women: body odor led them to matrimony and the blacks accepted them as whites: Almost whites because the Italian has much African in him, and his color is a dull pale."[17] Both learned and popular opinions point to miscegenation as an important factor in the diminution of the Afro-Argentine population. Socially and ideologically, interethnic unions were not frowned upon by the black population, given the negative status of blackness in society. Many willingly participated in the pigmentocracy that was established.

Self-Help

The impact of mutual aid societies upon the Afro-Argentine community and its advancement is debatable. In theory, these organizations

15. Marta B. Goldberg, "La población negra y mulata de la ciudad de Buenos Aires, 1810–1840," 99.

16. Elena F. S. de Studer, *La trata de negros en el Río de la Plata durante el siglo XVII*, 337.

17. Mariano G. Bosch, "Los negros de los abuelos," 25.

were sources of unity and positive ethnic identity. But in reality, their impact was at best marginal, except in a few cases. This was due to a number of factors. First of all, membership and participation were limited. Second, there were strict official rules governing the organization and function of the societies. Third, the level of internal struggle often did not allow for the organizations to carry out their missions.

Initially, Afro-Argentine organizations were not tightly scrutinized by government agencies, but this changed because of fear and distaste for black customs by some of the rulers of the society. Hence, as early as 1778, petitions were drafted to make the Afro-Argentine, free and slave, conform to what their roles were supposed to have been.

Afro-Argentines recognized early on that there was strength in numbers and that both religious and secular organizations would be necessary to assure their progress. One indication of these eighteenth-century efforts is a document directed to the King of Spain and signed by Andrés de Torres: *"Year 1785:* Document in which the blacks of Saint Baltazar Confraternity petition to build a chapel in which to celebrate their functions."[18]

The reply is positive and patronizing: "And the subjects finding themselves with the heavy yoke of slavery which they perpetually suffer, so in agreement giving infinite thanks to the All Powerful upon seeing themselves redeemed among Christians . . . the permission to build a chapel to saint Baltazar and Prayers so that in it slave and free brothers will gather on days of worship to pay homage to the All Powerful." The correspondence generated by the request on the part of Andrés Torres to build a site for the Saint Baltazar Brotherhood consists of approximately twenty pages. This demonstrates both the persistence necessary and the difficulty inherent in the system that blacks had to manipulate in an effort to gain some degree of self-determination.

Laws delineating the functioning of Afro-Argentine self-help societies were apparently formalized in 1827, when the *Political and Literary Chronicle of Buenos Aires* published a document regarding the "societies of black Africans established with permission of the authority with

18. Archivo General de la Nación, División Colonia, Sección Gobierno, Justicia 1785, Espediente 407, No. 445, Legado 17.

statement of their funds, lodging, and streets on which they exist, and the time they were authorized." The importance of this "relación" is that it institutionalized the societies and instituted rigid governmental control of the organization's activities. All were subsequently governed by the same rules approved by the authorities.

The objectives of these societies were indeed noble and consisted of six basic obligations. They were:

(1) Liberate with their funds those who are worthy of this honor through morality and industriousness.

(2) Care for the moral and practical education of the young people incorporated in the society.

(3) Help the projects of the associates, giving them instruments for their respective jobs, reintegrating their importance as stipulated.

(4) Assure that each member observes moral and productive conduct.

(5) Make once a year suffrage for the souls of the dead.

(6) The wealth of the societies is made up of the annual products of the farms, and of a monthly contribution of free members.[19]

Needless to say, these guidelines placed severe restrictions upon the Afro-Argentine societies by stipulating cradle-to-grave burdens upon the segment of the population least equipped to handle this type of social responsibility and economic pressure. Of the seven societies mentioned in the "relación," Cabunda, Bangala, Moros, Rubolo, Angolo, Conga, and Mina, only four, the Cabunda, Bangala, Conga, and Mina, existed twenty-five years later, and these were struggling.

Contrary to popular belief, there was not much harmony in the relationships between the different mutual aid societies. The evidence that

19. *Crónica política y literaria de Buenos Aires*, 2.

survives charting the course of the forty or so organizations presents the picture of organizations impacted adversely by internal bickering, war, and apathy. The Sociedad Marave/Marabe is a case in point. Founded in 1827, thirty years later it was at the point of disbanding because only four of the original members remained. Juana Sánchez, mother of the congregation, petitioned to the authorities for permission to hold the organization together: "because of the breakup of the Nation for military service rendered in the time of Rosas, Mother Juana Sánchez had taken charge of reinstituting the society, filling it again with different individuals who supported the idea."[20] She solidified the organization, many of whose members gave their lives in support of Rosas, until Juan Vásquez was elected president. The history of other black self-help organizations is similar.

Since the mutual aid societies were unable to do so, it was left up to the black press to assume a leadership role in the articulation of Afro-Argentine concerns to the larger society. Strength in numbers was their leitmotif. An editorial in *El Unionista* in 1877 entitled "Indiferencia" sums up the prevailing sentiment: "There are presently three mutual aid societies and among the three combined, the number does not reach two hundred members, despite the fact that our group is very numerous, so much so that if only one fourth of them would join the aforementioned associations each one could count on a thousand members, which would be enough, as it is known, for the three to have a prosperous life."[21]

El Unionista's call to arms did not go unheeded by La Protectora, a mutual aid society that had been founded by Eugenio Sar in July 1877 and that became the most effective black self-help organization in Buenos Aires, enduring well into the twentieth century. As he concludes his term as President of La Protectora in 1914, Tomás Castillo surmises: "I see surrounding our Protectora men from other times who were outside of the Society; I also see as a sign of progress the enrollment of more than two hundred associates who have begun to share

20. "Marabe," Archivo General de la Nación, División Gobierno Nacional—Policía, Sociedades Africanas 1845-1864.
21. *El Unionista* 1, no. 20 (30 de diciembre 1877): 1.

our work, and I see more, that the name of 'La Protectora' resonates in all of our society in general, as if announcing that the day is not far off when we can count in our ranks the majority of our social collective."[22] La Protectora had enjoyed limited success in unifying some segments of the Afro-Argentine population. However, the overall tendency was to wage individual battles on diverse fronts to stem the tide toward diminution of the black population.

Afro-Argentines and Literacy

The question of audience is inextricably bound to the publishing efforts of blacks in Argentina. For whom were the messages and works of Afro-Argentines intended? The majority of the black population was not literate, as one would expect from a people just removed from bondage, when various manifestations of their discourse began to appear.

The first national census in Argentina was taken in 1869, and literacy was one of the statistics surveyed. Jorge María Ramallo observes: "According to the *Census,* the level of instruction was very low. Of all the inhabitants, only 360,683 acknowledged knowing how to read and 312,011 how to write, which means that there was approximately 80 percent illiteracy."[23]

There are no exact statistics concerning the number of Afro-Argentines who were literate, semiliterate, or illiterate. However, there is evidence that there was a small group of individuals who were educated and assumed leadership roles in the area of social advancement. Since blacks were perceived of, first and foremost, as cheap labor sources, their education was not one of Argentine society's chief objectives. Nevertheless, as Andrews observes, some Afro-Argentines were afforded the opportunity to earn an education, especially in Buenos Aires:

> It is known that the city's Beneficent Society established a segregated school for mulatto and moreno students sometime around 1830, and in 1852 it opened two more segregated schools for black girls. These

22. Tomás Castillo, *La Protectora, Sociedad de Socorros Mutuos,* 7.
23. Jorge María Ramallo, *Historia Argentina fundamental,* 371.

two girls' schools continued to operate into the 1860s, containing at their height, in the 1850s, 17 percent of the city's female students. Though by 1853 the boys' schools were open to black students, informal discrimination prevented the Afro-Argentines from occupying an equal place in them. *La Crónica* of July 15, 1855, carried an article on the discriminatory treatment of blacks in Buenos Aires' public schools, to which one of the accused teachers retorted that since black children had to earn their living as domestic servants, they could never come to morning classes, and it was for this reason that they did so badly in school. The rector of the University of Buenos Aires expressed regret that as yet no black students had entered the university, to which he added his profound hopes that he might soon have the pleasure of teaching such students. As late as 1882, no black student had yet graduated from the university.[24]

The fact that there was a small number of Afro-Argentine writers and journalists at any given time did not deter them from articulating their social concerns and demanding respect as contributors to the intellectual life of the country. The audience of the black intellectuals was not the illiterate masses, but rather that semiliterate and literate segment of the population which was capable of reading, interpreting, and conveying their message to the less fortunate. Literate Afro-Argentines recognized early on that they were responsible for their own destiny and they did not wish to pass from history without leaving a meaningful documented trace.

The Press

The year 1852 was crucial for Afro-Argentines because of the defeat and exile to Europe of Juan Manuel Rosas. Until this point in history, they had played a key role in the development of that nation as slaves, freed persons, and soldiers who were significant forces in the wars of liberation and national conflicts. Black soldiers, men and women, were shock troops, cannon fodder for many Argentine *caudillos,* including Rosas, the most notorious manipulator and exploiter of all. With his demise in 1852, we see the beginning of the decline of black influence

---

24. George Reid Andrews, *The Afro-Argentines of Buenos Aires: 1800–1900,* 60.

and national impact as an ethnic group. Shortly thereafter, a law was passed (La Ley Avellaneda) that called for the colonization of Argentina with Europeans on a large scale. In 1852 there were approximately 1,000,000 Argentines; in 1869 there were 1,830,214; and in 1895 there were 3,954,911. In essence, the population, through immigration, had quadrupled in forty years. The strategy, "to govern is to populate"—with Europeans—had worked as Argentina aimed for a massive blood transfusion. The documented number of Argentines of African descent declined precipitously during this historical period. With the rise of the white population, there was a corresponding decline in Afro-Argentines in Buenos Aires, from 14,928 to 8,005, or from 26.1 percent of the population to 1.8 percent.

Afro-Argentines reacted immediately to official attempts to eliminate them from society. The most vocal and aware persons appear to be those affiliated with black periodicals whose stated purpose was to inform and to educate. Much of what we know about the participation in and contributions to Argentine society by blacks is documented in *Beneméritos de mi estirpe* (Outstanding members of my race), a book published by Jorge Miguel Ford in 1899. Ford's work has been plagiarized and anthologized by many but remains the most important source of documentation regarding the activities of important Afro-Argentines. It is from the periodicals and Ford that we get a true sense of community, of blacks determined to improve their lot through sacrifice and contributions to the nation.

The black press was very instrumental in the attempt to create an Afro-Argentine discourse—that is, a well-formulated and systematic treatment of the subjects of color and class. It articulated early on three of the major concerns of postcolonial discourse, that is, the press attempted to "invoke certain ways of thinking about language, about truth, about power, and about the interrelations between all three."[25] Initially, Afro-Argentines attempted to use their newspapers as instruments to raise the level of awareness about their plight and for empowerment, but they discovered that their versions of the truth were not shared by the majority who held the keys to power. In 1858,

25. Ashcroft, Griffith, and Tiffin, *The Empire Writes Back,* 167.

five years after the end of slavery, *El Proletario,* the earliest black newspaper which has survived to the present, not only recognized social inequities but called for "reparation for the evils we have suffered for such a long time and our advancement and well being and that of our children."[26] These muted voices of protest are prevalent throughout the three decades of black periodicals studied here, which include *La Broma, El Unionista, La Perla,* and *El Aspirante.*

The attitude of Afro-Argentine intellectuals toward their plight is summed up in an editorial, "La Educación," which appeared in *El Unionista* in 1877: "We are alone, in our country few are the men of value who are interested in our luck, before on the contrary many opposed our progress, and we will not advance from the subaltern condition in which our parents left us; except by educating ourselves and fighting united against our constant adversaries who believe that the black man does not have either heart or feelings that he is an entity subject to the same laws as other irrational beings, live, suffer and shut up."[27] Yes, the subaltern can speak, and they do so in a forceful manner. This dismal state of affairs of Afro-Argentines is reiterated by other publications that advocated black progress. There was a concerted effort by newspapers, journals, and writers to make known the intolerable conditions of Afro-Argentines during the years following abolition, with the intention of improving them. The outrage expressed at being treated as second-class citizens because of skin color is a constant theme of this alienated and dispossessed group. These attitudes were echoed by creative writers, many of whom were affiliated with the press.

The editorial "La Libertad," published in *La Broma* in 1879 and included here in its entirety, is one of the last periodical assessments of the plight of Afro-Argentines that has survived to the present:

> Liberty, Equality and Brotherhood, is the theme of all republican ideas because they are daughters of the pure sentiments of honorable men who work in favor of the general good. People who are able to show to the world without falsifying that theme, those are the happy people. But unfortunately they are few or none. The ideas of liberty,

26. *El Proletario* 1, no. 2 (24 de abril 1858): 1.
27. *El Unionista* 1, no. 20 (30 de diciembre 1877): 1.

equality, and brotherhood, only exist in the mind of the legislators upon creating the laws that must govern the people, but they go no further than there, as everyday we see it in our country.

Our Constitution does not make a distinction of race, nor position to authorize the guarantees and responsibilities that each child of the soil has. And nevertheless, the men charged with assuring respect and compliance with the Constitution, are the first to violate it. Beginning by excluding us from all right to aspire to any public position without remembering that in order for them to enjoy that right, we have been the first to abandon our families, and our home, to rush off to defend the homeland, when it has been offended by an enemy. When some *caudillo* has risen up against the established order, we have been the defenders of the constituted authorities. And what has been the payback? Hate, humiliation. And when we have invoked the Constitution as saving anchor for our rights they have responded to us with a sarcastic laugh. Equality in our country exists in form only. That is the freedom our class enjoys before the law.[28]

Ironically, this type of attitude regarding the treatment of Afro-Argentines is often denied. On the contrary, the consciousness-raising activities of the Afro-Argentine press are the products of a long history of social responsibility. In an editorial entitled "A New Era" commemorating the sixth appearance of *La Broma,* the reader is told

Before *La Broma* there could have existed other periodicals like *La Raza Africana, El Proletario, La Crónica, El Artesano, La Igualdad* and many others that have come afterwards, but—although we are humbled by immodest ones—none of them has reported the benefits of this one *(La Broma).* Because it exclusively, has become the faithful interpreter of the most transcendental questions that have occurred in the current century.[29]

For economic reasons, the Afro-Argentine press could not sustain itself. Nevertheless, it performed a great service by serving as a voice for the black community and placing its issues before the public. Without

28. *La Broma* 1, no. 23 (18 de diciembre 1879): 1.
29. *La Broma* 2d época (23 de diciembre 1881): 1.

its documented presence, we might still be asking the question of whether there were blacks in Argentina who were aware of their origin and presence.

From documents that have survived, it is apparent that the Afro-Argentine struggle for freedom, dignity, and self-determination paralleled that of blacks throughout the Americas. They waged a constant battle against biological extermination through miscegenation, as well as an ever-vigilant posture against those who would write them out of the national history. As a result, the Afro-Argentine version of what transpired in the Plate Estuary region is at odds with the official story.

Contributions of the black press, and the works of Elejalde, Mendizábal, Ezeiza, and other writers, are not included in standard histories of Argentine literature. Andrews, the historian, mentions their existence in his excellent study, but his focus is not literary. My task is twofold: as a literary historian—which is most important—I must, as Robert Spiller points out, "answer such questions as *How? When? Where? Why?* a work of literature exists or has existed and what its relationships are or were to other works of literature, and to the whole history of man as a sentient and social being."[30] As a literary critic, I must formulate an approach that will allow me to deal with the work on its own terms and not arrive with a set of theoretical and practical attitudes that would prohibit the writers from recognizing their own creations, given the opportunity.

Therefore, postcolonial criticism, which is not *the* answer to my theoretical dilemma, offers some viable options for the interpretation of the Afro-Argentine situation. Some would argue that Afro-Argentines never evolved to the postcolonial stage. Instead, they remained in a state of internal colonialism until their ultimate demise. Such an attitude negates the diversity of blacks in Argentina as well as their unending struggle for equality and recognition for their accomplishments. In his discussion of the "Survival of Culture," Homi K. Bhabha, a prominent critic, writes that "a range of contemporary critical theories suggest that it is from those who have suffered the sentence of history—subjugation,

---

30. Robert Spiller, "Literary History," in James Thorpe, ed., *The Aims and Methods of Scholarship in Modern Languages and Literatures,* 43.

domination, diaspora, displacement—that we learn our most enduring lessons for living and thinking. There is even a growing conviction that the affective experience of social marginality—as it emerges in noncanonical cultural forms—transforms our critical strategies." The reconstruction of the Afro-Argentine literary presence is but the first step in an examination of the broader impact of black culture in Argentina. This may involve the reevaluation of some critical assumptions but, in the final analysis, some of us will have a better understanding of that country and of ourselves.

CHAPTER ONE
The Romantic Mode in Afro-Argentine Letters

The majority of Afro-Argentine writers whose works have survived to the present belonged to the "romantic" and "creole" generations that spanned a time frame of approximately eighty years: 1830–1910. Black romantics wrote, for the most part, within the literary conventions prevalent in that country. In his definition of this movement, Enrique Anderson Imbert, the Argentine literary historian, explains: "Within the vast thematics of world romanticism, the most typical themes of Spanish America were the natural countryside, human types, the way of living in different social circumstances and history."[1] Afro-Argentine writers such as Mateo Elejalde and Horacio Mendizábal reflect the aforementioned concerns, which vary from the universal to the local in their poetry. They further bend romantic conventions to interpret the plight of the black population.

Thematically and stylistically, Afro-Argentine romantic poets conform to the same standards as their counterparts. According to Anderson Imbert, "The emphasis upon emotion, the uncertainty of thought and the carelessness in writing also remained recorded in romantic syntax. The preferred verse forms were the sonnet and the *romance.* Metrics were enriched, above all in strophic combinations. With notable frequency romantic poets, to give variety to a composition and to blend the movement of themes, combined different methods." The incorporation of emotional, sometimes personal, experiences into their poetry is a common phenomenon in Afro-Argentine poets who are concerned with love, liberty, and social justice. Just as other romantic poets, their

---

1. Enrique Anderson Imbert, *Historia de la literatura hispanoamericana,* 239–40.

works reflect metric variety and incorporate a mixture of prose and poetry in some of their contributions.

However, in spite of conformation to canonical dictates, Afro-Argentines expressed sentiments of alienation and psychological marginalization caused by the historical and political forces that created and maintained their position as marginalized, oppressed subjects.

Elejalde

The basic characteristics of Argentine romanticism as outlined by Anderson Imbert, such as concern for the countryside, human types, and social customs, are prevalent in Elejalde and Mendizábal, to cite two examples. But what distinguishes these two authors from classic Argentine romanticist writers such as Echeverría, Mármol, and Hernández is that blacks become the *subject* rather than the *object* of the discourse. Afro-Argentines in traditional, canonized works of the aforementioned authors, like *El matadero* (1836), *Amalia* (1852), and *Martín Fierro* (1872/1879) are denigrated, marginalized characters. The counterdiscourse of Elejalde and Mendizábal moves blacks from the margins to the center with the idea of resisting false interpretations of the African presence in that country. They are therefore within the thematic and ideological constraints associated with the postcolonial epoch.

While Mendizábal published two volumes of poetry, the contributions of Elejalde, whose dates of birth and death are unknown, are found in the pages of *La Broma*. His poetry, which covers the thematic spectrum, appeared between February 1881 and December 1882. During this time span, the reader is witness to an accomplished poet well schooled in local and worldly topics. The two dozen poems published in the periodical *La Broma* by Elejalde can be divided thematically into love, nature, life/death, solitude/alienation, and social concerns.

Although no critical reaction to Elejalde's poetry is available in mainstream publications, he was read and appreciated by his peers. A rare written appraisal of his work appeared in the "Variedades" section of *La Broma* in March 1882. The anonymous "C" writes:

> Ay! Your heart hides in a sanctuary an echo for all the sounds and in them you inspire your strophes, awakening in each one of them, a

new emotion like any trophy of tears, covers the landscape of life with the shroud of death and discovers in the world horizons impregnated with faith, love and hope.

Espronceda, Mármol, Petrarch, Valera, Byron, Dante and a thousand others with the torch of immortal genius, illuminate your path and give hope to your spirit, mark your course, disdaining the egoism of humanity, and time in your swift career, will show you the beaten path leaving the twists of thought but harvesting the brilliance of your idea. Forward![2]

This individual not only delineates the basic characteristics of Elejalde's poetry but also places him alongside the outstanding romantic poets of the Western tradition. As a romantic, Elejalde is expected to be emotional, deal with life-and-death issues, and interpret basic human sentiments. The critic also stresses Elejalde's basic humanity as well as his ability to convert sentiment to verse.

Half of Elejalde's poems are devoted to the theme of love and include outstanding selections such as "A Ella" (To Her), "Ausente" (Absence), and "Suspiros" (Sighs). "To Her" is representative, in tone and style, of all the love poetry of Elejalde:

Soft music, a sublime note
Tender harmony of a chaste love,
Filled with life, filled with enchantment
Thus is the beauty of your sweet voice.

Sky without clouds—white stars
Glittering sun rays
Beautiful dawn a happy day
Thus are your eyes my love.

Timid rose of the morning
Filled with inebriating nectar
Thus is your luxuriant and pure mouth
Filled with aroma like a flower . . .
Tender sighs your soul inhales

2. Anon., "Mateo Elejalde," *La Broma* (9 de marzo 1882): 1.

Tender laments your heart
I who understand your sweet complaint
while hearing your moan of love.

Brilliant star of my happiness,
Heavenly image that my soul created . . .
Divine goddess, timid and beautiful,
You are the angel of my illusion!

(Música suave, nota sublime,
Tierna armonía de un casto amor,
Llena de vida, llena de encanto
Así es hermosa tu dulce voz.

Cielo sin nubes—blancos luceros
Resplandeciente rayos del sol,
Aurora bella un feliz día
Así mi vida tus ojos son.

Tímida rosa de la mañana
Llena de néctar embriagador.
Así es tu boca lozana y pura
Llena de aroma, como una flor . . .
Tiernos suspiros enhala tu alma,
Tiernos lamentos tu corazón
Yo que comprendo su dulce queja
Al escucharte gimo amor.

Fúlgida estrella de mi ventura,
Célica imágen que mi alma creó . . .
Diosa divina, tímida y bella,
Eres el ángel de mi ilusión!)[3]

The poem is dedicated to the feminine ideal as the real and imagined woman is interpreted as an integral component of the natural and celestial orders. This poem and the other traditional ones illustrate the "double voice" of Elejalde that is analogous to other Afro-Hispanic

3. *La Broma* (3 de febrero 1881): 2.

writers. To be accepted as an exponent of the Argentine romantic mode, Elejalde had to demonstrate his command of classic themes and forms before incorporating the black dimension of his consciousness into his poetry. Elejalde is then able to deal with the canon and to exorcise his personal demons.

A feeling of alienation and loss permeates the poetry of Elejalde and reaches its maximum expression in "¡Soledad!" (Solitude). Death is the predominant motif in this selection, which combines the cosmic and the mundane:

> I hear the sad voice of the bell
>   Which announces the prayer
> And each echo that vibrates, resounds
>   Within my heart.
>
> Now the day is dying; silently it reaches
>   To the dubious light
> Of the pale sunset which advances
>   The lonely cross
>
> At the foot of a hill resplendent
>   In lush greenness
> Where a thousand flowers, breathing, exhale
>   An inebriating aroma.
>
> Over there I direct my uncertain step,
>   With my yearning breast
> As if I were searching in that tomb for
>   A kiss from my lover!
>
> It is that solitude, which reigns all around,
>   The mysterious calm,
> Of heavenly inexplicable happiness
>   Fills my soul!
>
> My voice then rises up, emotional
>   In fervent prayer
> Alongside the silent tomb,
>   Of the lonely cross!
>
> Oh, solitude! I am in ecstasy in your calm!
>   Beautiful illusions

Swirl in my mind, like a swarm
  Of winged butterflies!

Of ineffable anxiety, sobbing
  The heart beats
And in a world without name; indescribable
  My spirit is restless!

I dream of another more beautiful hour
  Longing of my life!
I dream of the future which smiles on me,
  About the woman I love!

Oh solitude! You revive my memories,
  My dead illusions!
And I feel a thousand hopes reborn
  From their dead ashes!

(Oigo la triste voz de la campana
  Que anuncia la oración,
Y cada eco que vibra, repercute
  Dentro mi corazón.

Ya muere el día; se alza silenciosa
  A la dudosa luz
Del pálido crepúsculo que avanza
  La solitaria cruz.

Al pie de una colina engalanada
  De lozano verdor,
Donde mil flores, suspirando, exhalan
  Aroma embriagador.

Allí dirijo mi pisada incierta,
  Con el pecho anhelante,
Cual si fuera a buscar en esa tumba
  ¡Un beso de mi amante!

Y es que la soledad, que reina en torno,
  La misteriosa calma,
De celestial, inexplicable dicha,
  ¡Llena mi alma!

Mi voz entonces se alza, conmovida,
  En ferviente plegaria,
Al borde de la tumba silenciosa,
  ¡De la cruz solitaria!

¡Oh! ¡soledad! ¡yo me extasio en tu calma!
  Ilusiones hermosas
Revolan en mi mente, cual enjambre
  ¡De aladas mariposas!

De ansiedad inefable, sollozando,
  El corazón palpita
Y en un mundo sin nombre, indescriptible,
  ¡Mi espíritu se agita!

Yo sueño con otra hora más hermosa.
  ¡Anhelo de mi vida!
Sueño en el porvenir que me sonrie,
  ¡En la mujer querida!

¡Oh! ¡soledad! tú avivas mis recuerdos,
  Mis ilusiones muertas!
Y siento renacer mil esperanzas
  ¡De sus cenizas yertas!)[4]

The poet's sense of estrangement is compounded by the overriding images of death and desolation, which contrast the living with the defunct. The poet's loss is physical as well as spiritual.

Elejalde's romantic musings do not divert his attention from the plight of Afro-Argentines. In fact, one of the first poems he published is entitled "La redención" (Redemption) and deals with ethnicity and discriminatory practices against blacks. It is both a call to arms and an exercise in consciousness raising:

Already the announced hour has sounded
During which an oppressed race

4. *La Broma* (18 de marzo 1882): 1.

Begins to enter a life
Of sublime redemption;
Finally . . . the pale night
Which covered our sky,
Announces to us a beautiful day,
Of sweet resurrection.

Let's inspire ourselves also;
Yes, let's lift up our heads,
Let's receive its brilliance
And in its changing colors,
Let our ideas be tempered,
By the rays the sun sends
And let the cold soul encourage
The sparkle of your temple.

Let us follow hurriedly
The broad road
Fighting with destiny
And with diversity itself;
Let us continue forward always,
Filled with fertile longing,
Because in this world also
There is posterity . . .

Let us continue forward always,
Don't let barriers stop us,
And let our guiding light be,
Swift thought:
That winged messenger
Who crosses spaces and clouds
And who even clings to the heavens
Lifting up the soul to God.

Yes, forward—let's lift up
Our eyes, haughty
Let not the outlaw discourage us
With his fury without equal.
Let's fight with a strong arm,
Remembering the sweet name

Of the Eternal Son of Man
Who saved humanity . . .

Forward, yes forward,
Each time with more persistence . . .
Eternal hate for ignorance,
Love for education!
Divine education,
Unextinguishable light
And heavenly messenger
Of sublime redemption.

(Ya sonó la hora anunciada
En que una raza oprimida
Empieza a entrar en la vida
De sublime redención;
Por fin . . . la pálida noche
Que nuestro cielo cubría,
Nos anuncia un bello día,
De dulce resurrección.

Sí; levantemos la frente,
Recibamos sus fulgores
Y en sus cambiantes colores,
Inspirémonos también;
Que templen nuestras ideas,
Los rayos que el sol envia
Y alienten al alma fría
Los destellos de su sien.

Sigamos apresurados
El anchuroso camino,
Luchando con el destino
Y la misma adversidad;
Sigamos siempre adelante,
Lleno de anhelo fecundo,
Que también en este mundo
Hay una posteridad . . .

Sigamos siempre adelante,
No nos detengan barreras,

Y sea nuestra lumbrera,
El pensamiento veloz:
Ese alado mensajero
Que cruza espacios y nubes
Y que hasta los cielos sube
Elevando de alma a Dios.

Sí, adelante—levantemos
Nuestra mirada, altaneros
No nos abata el pampero
Con su furia sin igual,
Luchemos con fuerte brazo,
Recordando el dulce nombre
Del Hijo Eterno Del Hombre
Que salvó la humanidad . . .

Adelante, ¡sí! adelante,
Cada vez con más constancia . . .
Odio eterno a la ignorancia,
Amor a la educación!
A la educación divina,
Inestinguible lumbrera
Y celeste mensajera
De sublime redención.)[5]

The poem's initial stanza postulates a dialectical tension that will structure subsequent verses. The motif of "our time has come" charts a course from oppression to redemption to resurrection. The dichotomy between "pale night" and "pretty day" underscores the push for societal change. "Paleness" refers to the majority culture whose attitudes and practices have oppressed blacks for centuries.

In "Redemption," Elejalde articulates his basic aspirations for the advancement of Afro-Argentines within the romantic conventions of rebellion and resistance. Movement in the poem is from oppression to redemption through collective action. "Lift up," "Be inspired," "Move forward," "Let's fight" are motivational motifs modeled upon the black

5. *La Broma* (3 de febrero 1881): 2.

struggle as well as that of Christ. Persistence and education are components of the historical Afro-Argentine struggle and are ways to ensure
future advancement. Elejalde, like the black journalists, is concerned
with the "place" of Afro-Argentines. Without struggle and resistance,
there is no progress.

The importance of Elejalde's call for redemption and the uplifting
of Afro-Argentines is that it comes, during the 1880s, at precisely the
time when the forces of Civilization (White/European) are making their
strongest push to eliminate the elements of Barbarism (Blacks/Indians)
from the national ethos. From Juan Alberdi's *Bases y puntos de partida
para la organización política argentina* (Foundations and starting
points for Argentine political organization, 1852) to Domingo Faustino
Sarmiento's *Conflictos y armonías de las razas en América* (Conflicts
and agreements of the races in America, 1883), intense efforts were
waged to downplay the significance of the black presence in Argentina
and to eliminate them as an ethnic component. Elejalde's poem is both
a reaction to racist ideology and a call for national unity. "Redemption"
is, at best, wishful thinking.

Mendizábal: *Primeros versos* (First verses)

Horacio Mendizábal published two volumes of poetry: *Primeros
versos* (First verses, 1865) and *Horas de meditación* (Hours of meditation, 1869). Critical reactions in Argentina to Mendizábal's works have
varied. According to Ricardo Rojas, Mendizábal "lacked personality,
and also true poetic skill. Mendizábal's muse—if I can express myself
this way—moved from the satirical to the elegiac, from the epic to the
didactic, via a path of faltering rhythms, in which the poorly measured
verse is not missing. Evidently, Mendizábal was not a poet."[6] Rojas's
attitude toward Mendizábal is ambivalent, since at the same time he
is denying that Mendizábal is a poet, he points out that Mendizábal
"cultivated the most varied lyric forms: the madrigal, the ode, the silva,
the sonnet, the acrostic, the dolora. His verses permit his character to
intervene, his experience: he praised the home, love and the country."

6. Ricardo Rojas, *Historia de la literatura argentina: los modernos,* 362.

Since Rojas does not delineate the characteristics of good poetry, one must assume that his evaluation of Mendizábal is based upon factors other than the texts.

A more balanced view of Mendizábal is presented by Ricardo Rodríguez Molas, who, while agreeing with Rojas that Mendizábal lacks "personalidad artística" and "ingenio poético," recognizes that the writer's responsibility entails much more than writing beautiful verses. Rodríguez Molas observes: "It was the race which stirred in his pen, the rancor of the slave who had gained his freedom during the dawn of the homeland. The poet suffered the condemnation and the isolation that numerous whites imposed upon the grandsons and sons of those slaves. Color weighed heavily upon the individual in the aristocratic society of Buenos Aires."[7] Mendizábal chose to make some of his poetry a socially responsible and aesthetically pleasing vehicle depicting the plight of the Afro-Argentine population. On the other hand, as a romantic poet, his work is comparable in quality to those of his generation. My comparative readings of representative poetic texts published by mainstream Argentine writers of this period reveal no superiority in terms of overall quality and skill when compared to the works of Mendizábal. This is certainly true when one considers books like *Poesías* (1865) by José María Zuviría, *Ráfagas poéticas* (1866) by Mario A. Pelliza, *Poesías* (1869) by Juan María Gutiérrez, and *Poesías* (1869) by Florencio Balcarel. Yet Mendizábal is not mentioned alongside these writers whose works have gone down in history as "hechos culturales" (cultural events). Mendizábal's approach, too, was that of a double-voiced artist who was aware of his audience and his circumstances.

From the comments of Rojas and Rodríguez Molas, it is apparent that Mendizábal was a talented and multifaceted poet. Adept at manipulating the various poetic tropes and rhetorical figures, from local color to mythology, the poet decided early to use his verse as an arm for social reform, an attitude that prevailed throughout his poetry. Mendizábal, who lived from 1847 to 1871, when he perished during the yellow fever epidemic, practiced what he preached as he was exposed to the

7. Ricardo Rodríguez Molas, "Horacio Mendizábal: poeta de color en el Buenos Aires del siglo XIX," 167.

virus while helping others. His tendency to combine the social and the aesthetic is apparent early on in his career.

The poems of *First Verses* follow classic romantic motifs in their form and substance. They include numerous allusions to mythology, beauty, human vices, the mother, the family, the homeland, and other standard poetic motifs of the Western tradition. This collection contains verses devoted to almost any imaginable topic, and clearly demonstrates the sophistication of Mendizábal and his firm grounding in Argentine and European cultures. Alongside romantic motifs like love and the night, the poet devotes a great deal of time to freedom—both individual and collective. "La libertad" (Liberty) is indicative of this tendency:

> That with a firm stare and which boldly
> Raises its head filled with pride,
> That which softly makes life pleasing
> Electrifying for us its brilliance;
>
> That for which our parents fought,
> That heavenly Goddess of kindness,
> That which our mothers loved so much
> It is sublime, beautiful Liberty!
>
> That upon which your noble foot treads
> Against the despot, the oppressed rises up,
> That for which so much blood spills,
> It's called Liberty. A dear name!
>
> You, oppressed people cry out
> The holy shout "Liberty!" . . .
> From where the coward's terror does not reach
> The noble man's heroism arrives.
>
> (Esa de firme vista y que atrevida
> Alza la frente llena de altivez,
> Esa que suave hace agradar la vida
> Electrizándonos su brillantez;
>
> Esa por quien pelearon nuestros padres,
> Esa celeste Diosa de bondad,
> Esa que amaron tanto nuestras madres
> Es la sublime, ¡bella Libertad!

Esa que pisa con su noble planta
Al déspota, levanta al oprimido,
Esa por quien se vierte sangre tanta,
Se llama Libertad. ¡Nombre querido!

Vosotros, pueblos oprimidos lanza
El sacrosanto grito "¡Libertad!" . . .
Que do el cobarde en su terror no alcanza
Llega del noble la heroicidad.)[8]

Anaphora with "esa" underscores the poem's basic thrust—liberty or death. "Liberty" is structured around a series of binary oppositions involving despotism/oppression in contrast to freedom. The poet's historical awareness is evident in verses such as "That for which our parents fought" and "That which our mothers loved so much." In true romantic fashion, the exaltation of "Liberty" occurs in a conflictive image cluster extolling heroism over cowardice. Mendizábal's cry for freedom is not limited to the Afro-Argentine situation but encompasses the experiences of enslaved and colonized peoples everywhere.

Mendizábal dedicates two poems to the Afro-Argentine military hero Coronel José María Morales. Morales (1818–1894) is profiled in Jorge Miguel Ford's *Outstanding Members of My Race* as a multitalented individual: "he was an industrialist, musician, poet, military man, politician and above all, this most honored of professions, an unwavering patriot who shined for the commitment to the cause of his creed; guardian of the rights of his country."[9] The positive virtues of these leadership positions occupied by Morales are extolled by Mendizábal in "¡Alerta!" (Alert!) and "Conmemoración de la Batalla de Cepeda" (Commemoration of the Battle of Cepeda).

In these two poems, the heroism displayed by Morales against foreign aggression, as a fighter against the tyranny of Rosas, in the war against Paraguay, and in the subsequent internecine struggles within Argentina

8. Horacio Mendizábal, *Primeros versos,* 5–6. Subsequent references will appear in the text as *PV.*
9. Jorge Miguel Ford, *Beneméritos de mi estirpe,* 50.

constitute the subject matter. "Alert" is a call to arms for action against Spain if it invades Peru and a warning that Spain will suffer the same fate as in a previous war:

> Remember the renowned victories
> Of Ayacucho, Maipu and Junín,
> Remember the splendid glories,
> Where my forefathers found out how to die.

> (Recordad las insignes victorias
> De Ayacucho, de Maipu y Junín,
> Recordad las espléndidas glorias,
> Do mis padres supieron morir.) (*PV,* 33)

Historically, from the poet's perspective, Argentines have been willing to pay the ultimate price for freedom and are determined not to accept recolonization from Spain or any other country. Not to be overlooked in this nationalistic moment is the role Afro-Argentines played in battles determining the nation's destiny.

"Commemoration of the Battle of Cepeda" was written five years after that encounter, in which Morales was an active participant. The poet issues a disclaimer that he will not name, directly, any of the participants, but a strong image of Morales emerges:

> A bright day it was, sir, how brave
> The strong arm of a happy warrior,
> Powerful and towering,
> In combat rough, frightful,
> A fatal blow, horrible discharge
> Against his rival, who fought for the rewards.

> (Un lustro hoy há, señor, que valeroso
> El abrazo fuerte de feliz guerrero,
> Pujante y altanero,
> En el combate rudo, pavoroso,
> Golpe fatal, horrendo descargaba
> A su rival, que el lauro disputaba.) (*PV,* 72)

Morales is clearly the poetic subject and exhibits most of the qualities of valor embodied in the real-life hero. The poet evokes the sights and sounds of battle by providing a blow-by-blow account of the action, much of it from the perspective of Morales:

> The voice of command is heard
> From the warrior who dispatches
> The orders, adorned with medals
> Powerful weapons of the haughty Mars;
> And on his swift steed
> Reviews the huge, brave line
> And the steel reflects deathly fear,
> And in its tranquil surrounding
> He extends his noble and calm look,
> Extends the look to his army, which right away
> Is guided to war glory.

> (Se oye la voz de mando
> Del guerrero que imparte
> Las órdenes, de lauros adornado
> Fúlgidas armas del altivo Marte;
> Y en su corcel hinnible
> Corre la grande, valerosa fila
> Y el hierro luce funeral temible,
> Y en su redor tranquila
> Tiende la vista noble y sosegada,
> Tiende la vista a su legión, que presto
> Es a la gloria bélica guiada.) (PV, 73)

There are allusions to both classical myth—"Marte" (Mars), god of war, and "Febo" (Apollo), god of wisdom—and to Argentine reality in the poet's negative presentation of the *gaucho* (decrepit, trash), who compose much of the opposition to Morales and his troops. The nationalistic fervor demonstrated by the poet, which is a fundamental characteristic of romanticism, is invoked to present harmony and unity.

The presentations of José María Morales by Ford and Mendizábal are significant in the creation of an Afro-Argentine discourse, albeit within the constraints of romanticism. Morales does not appear in standard Argentine histories analyzing the role of the military in the development of that nation. He, like many other black soldiers, served the country well and was forgotten. Morales' exploits are brought to life again through the power of the poet to delve into the *intrahistoria* of the Afro-Argentine.

The passage of time and its impact upon the individual is another concern of Horacio Mendizábal. Again, this concept is treated within the broader classical frame of "tempus fugit" and ultimately related to the individual situation of the poet. On the occasion of his eighteenth birthday, the poetic voice takes stock of the world in which the poet lives and is not satisfied with what he perceives. The classic "ubi sunt" motif is the point of departure for his incursion into myth and reality. Eighteen years mark chronologically the passage from innocence to maturity ("Oh! angelic childhood; you abandoned me and left cruel pain in your place?") The device of the rhetorical question underscores the ironic situation as the poet escapes to another realm:

> Will my future be to grieve all alone,
> Will it be from the god Apollo,
> By ruining his lyre
> Who in my head explodes horrendous anger?
> Which Muses will it be? . . . Where?
> Thus lightly
> Goes your delirium, my downcast mind?
>
> (¿Mi futuro será plañir tan solo,
> Será del dios Apolo,
> Por estropear su lira,
> Que en mi cabeza estalla horrenda ira?
> ¿Será qué Musas? . . . ¿Dónde,
> Así ligeramente,
> Va tu delirio, mi abatida mente?) (*PV,* 75)

In his contemplative mood, the poet implores Apollo, Greco-Roman god of the wisdom of oracles, to help solve the dilemma of his future existence because he realizes that the past cannot be recaptured. The poet, in his fantasy, creates a harmonious world where old and young embrace each other. Blacks are not left out of the equation:

> There, the black who is born
> On the beach of burning sand,

Without the iron chain
Of the vile trafficker, a rude awakening,
Enjoys pleasing happiness
Enjoys, like everybody, without misfortune!

(Allí, el negro que nace
Sobre las playas de quemante arena,
Sin que férrea cadena
De traficante vil, ruda amenace,
Goza plácida dicha
Goza, cual todos, sin haber desdicha!) (*PV,* 76)

The poet creates a romantic vision of an idealized world that is a mere abstraction of the real one. He realizes in the end that he is faced with a world of hate and suffering. The black, due to past history, will bear the brunt of many of society's ills. The poet, as he matured, became predictably more isolated from Argentine society, a situation that reaches its apex in "Mi canto" (My song), Mendizábal's affirmation of self-worth, and which will shortly be discussed.

Horas de meditación (Hours of meditation)

In the introduction to *Hours of Meditation,* Horacio Mendizábal reiterates his position as a poet and proponent of justice and equality for all humans. Mendizábal believes that poetry has a social function as well as an aesthetic one: "Poetry is destined to lift up from its misery a destitute race, condemned to slavery and servility, to moral and material debasement."[10] Then, through a series of rhetorical questions, the poet scrutinizes the social and religious contexts of the Afro-Argentine:

How does one not feel pain before the misfortune of a sister race, sister before God and before reason?
How does one not tremble before the insult and the wicked humiliation that the white race casts on our soil upon the colored race, my race?

10. Horacio Mendizábal, *Horas de meditación,* 17. Subsequent references will appear in the text as *HM.*

> How in our century does one say to a man to his face: "Nigger! You will work for me, you will be mine, my slave, my thing—I AM YOUR MASTER!"
>
> How does one say to a person face to face: mulatto! You are a criminal, because your face is dark! Riff-raff! You do not have a homeland, except dying for it defending my interests; mulatto! I will not educate you so that you will never lift up your head where I raise it.
>
> The poet with a heart, the man who feels, he who is a true Christian does not have to articulate such iniquity; the priest of liberty has to lift up his voice in support of the exiled race, of that accused Isaac, downcast and humiliated to the point of degradation.
>
> The Catholic priest will not come to your aid because Catholicism is based upon obscurity, in the clouds, based upon ignorance: it will not raise its voice in support of my race as it has not raised it until now, because it is aristocratic *par excellence,* and for it men are not its brothers but its slaves; they say it: they are the sheep of its flock. (*HM,* 17–18)

Horacio Mendizábal begins *Hours of Meditation* with the strongest condemnation, in print, of racism by an Afro-Argentine poet. The lack of compassion, the inability of the majority culture to perceive the black as anything but the perpetual Other, exacerbates the rage expressed by Mendizábal. The master-slave dialectic condemns the Afro-Argentine to existence at the margins without hope of functioning at the social center. Mendizábal not only condemns racism but also launches an unprecedented criticism of Catholicism and its complicity with the social status quo. The poet views himself as a "poet of the heart," a "true Christian," a "priest of liberty" who stands in stark contrast to the aristocratic complicity of Catholicism.

Referring further along in the introduction to the example of the Haitian revolution that culminated in 1804, the poet laments: "One American nation sustains a gigantic war in defense of the destitute race. Let's imitate its example, and if in the Argentine Republic there are not material chains for the colored man, there is disdain, insult, humiliation by the white who spits in his face, who hates him" (*HM,* 20). Mendizábal appeals to the Christian decency of the Argentines to change attitudes and to help blacks realize their full potential. He implores the poets to serve as examples in the process of uplifting Afro-Argentines: "Poets, you who seek liberty, who pay homage to justice, defend that unfortunate race and you will be blessed."

Not only, from the poet's perspective, did God create all humans with the same obligations, rights, passions, feelings, faith, and hope, but also wars have been fought to ensure equal protection under the law: "The May Revolution proclaimed the principles of equality, liberty and brotherhood; but these noble principles must be practiced before the law and before society, not offending the man of color, not scorning him, nor forgetting him" (*HM*, 22). Mendizábal's rhetoric is very much in tune with the discourse of Afro-Argentine journalists who, at odds with the official story regarding their plight, hoped to use the media as an instrument for progress.

Toward the end of this introduction, the poet seems to realize that there is not much hope that profound changes will be made in favor of Afro-Argentines in the society because of the official attitude denying their existence and importance: "While lamenting the grave errors of the society in which we live, for which our color constitutes a crime, while measuring the separation of one class from another, the misfortune of one and the pride of the other, I abandoned this atmosphere of corruption, going to breathe the perfumed air of our flowery countryside" (*HM*, 23–24). This metaphorical escape is not in keeping with the poetic practice of Horacio Mendizábal since he proceeds, in *Hours of Meditation,* to engage society in a consciousness-raising dialogue.

In addition to poems devoted to classic Roman myths, *Hours of Meditation* contains poems in Italian, poems translated from French to Spanish, and a theatrical work entitled "Mujer celosa: drama original en tres actos" (Jealous woman: original drama in three acts). Mendizábal demonstrates his awareness of the broader Afro-American experience in poems like "Plácido" and "Lincoln."

"Plácido" is dedicated to the Cuban poet Gabriel de la Concepción Valdés (1804–1844), who was executed on June 28, 1844, after being charged with conspiring to free the slaves and gain independence for Cuba from Spain in the "Conspiración de la Escalera."[11] In the poem, Plácido is referred to as the "noble bard of black countenance." In this poetic homage, Plácido's life's trajectory is recreated

11. An excellent discussion of Plácido is presented by Richard Jackson in chapter 3 of *Black Writers in Latin America,* 36–44.

from birth to death with emphasis upon his rebellious and inspirational nature. Plácido's noble presence is maintained even in death:

> The discharge sounded . . . but heaven wished
> that all were extraordinary and large
> in the poet of the black countenance.
> Bullets respect him—All remain silent
> before the crude sinister spectacle,
> and amongst the smoke and blood of the victims
> The sad prisoner raises his head.
> Goodbye, goodbye he proclaimed, I leave this world.

> (La descarga sonó . . . mas quiso el cielo
> que todo fuese extraordinario y grande
> en el poeta del semblante negro.
> Las balas le respetan—Todos callan
> ante el crudo espectáculo siniestro,
> y entre el humo y la sangre de las víctimas
> Levanta la cabeza el triste reo.
> Adios, adios, clamó, parto del mundo.) (*HM*, 75)

The poet looks to international black heroes as examples to alleviate some of the oppression encountered in the Argentine situation. Plácido is elevated to mythic proportions because he was willing to sacrifice himself for the greater goal of the liberation of black people.

This universalization of the black struggle for liberation is continued in the sonnet devoted to Abraham Lincoln, who is credited with freeing U.S. slaves. Lincoln is presented as a true heroic model whose example has uplifted black people worldwide:

> Who was it, tell me, the innocent martyr
> Terror of slave traffickers and strongmen
> Before whom one hundred castles fell
> To the rude assault of his unconquered people?

> Who is the big valiant democrat
> Who broke the slave chains
> And while breaking to bits forever their links

Lowered disturbed his inspired head?

Lincoln! Lincoln! he was the powerful one
Who lifted up from the dust an oppressed race
Feeling the aggrieved prize in his heart.

May the cruel tyrant find treachery
When certain defeat threatens him
With the bloody blade in his right hand.

(¿Quién fue, decidme, el mártir inocente
Terror de traficantes y caudillos,
Ante el que se postaron cien castillos
Al rudo asalto de su invicta gente?

¿Quién el grande demócrata valiente
Que del esclavo quebrantó los grillos,
Y al trozar para siempre sus anillos
Dobló angustiado la inspirada frente?

Lincoln! Lincoln! él fué quien poderoso
Del polvo alzara una anijida raza,
Sintiendo en premio traspasado el pecho.

Que el tirano cruel halla alevoso
Cuando cierta derrota le amenaza
En el puñal sangriento su derecho.) (*HM*, 369)

The rhetorical question in the first two quartets underscores the
image of Abraham Lincoln as an enigmatic figure—an innocent martyr
but yet valiant with the knowledge of how to exercise power. The
ultimate beneficiaries are blacks in the United States. By comparing
the situation of his counterparts in Cuba and the United States, the
poet has a frame of reference with which to assess his own situation in
Argentina. This is the focus of "My Song."

"My Song," Mendizábal's most quoted poem, first appeared in *Hours
of Meditation.* It is useful, however, to see how he was perceived
by Ford, who included "My Song" as an exemplary poetic expression
in *Outstanding Members of My Race,* Ford's profiles of meritorious
Afro-Argentines. Ford maintains that Mendizábal "was not a giant in his

conceptions, no!" and that he was not of the same caliber of Echevarría or Mármol, outstanding romantic writers. Ford does, however, pay tribute to Mendizábal's contributions:

> Horacio Mendizábal had through his lineage a distinct, exceptional lute; the ideas which sprung forth in his imagination had no other school than those of his suffering and these generated his songs, without form many times, without fragrance if necessity requires it; but always tempered under the *ombú* of pain, of the fatal impressionism which the heart produces from the vulture who devours its prey. For that reason when at 19 years of age when his first verses appeared it was evident in them the defect in form and perhaps the sacrifice of the idea; but not to such a degree that would take from him the merit of a juvenile essay to which public indulgence favored with the spirit and dissimulation finding in their author a mine of metal which the passage of time would be in charge of polishing and giving greatness.[12]

While Ford does not lavish praise upon Mendizábal, he does recognize that the poet's work has a profound relationship to the society of which he forms a part. In addition, there has been an evolution, a more profound awareness, by Mendizábal of issues glossed over in *First Verses* that are now at the core of *Hours of Meditation.* Central to this new attitude is the issue of Afro-Argentine existence that is the theme of "My Song."

The first three stanzas of "My Song" contain standard romantic bird imagery, but establish a basic contradiction between the swan and the black bird with whom the poet identifies: "Swans of grandiose, colossal plumage, / I am the poor blackbird of the flowers, / The one who isolated, prefers its odors . . ." The poet builds upon the isolation metaphor, transferring it from birds to humans. In the fourth stanza, the posture is

> I am isolated in the midst of men,
> Isolated in a living society,
> Where I see brilliant names,

---

12. Ford, *Beneméritos,* 60.

Their titles, greatness and fame,
Also their misery and weakness.

(Aislado estoy en medio de los hombres,
Aislado en una viva sociedad,
De la que veo los brillantes nombres,
Sus títulos, grandezas y renombres,
Y también su miseria y su maldad.) (*HM*, 60)

The poet undermines the classic scene created in the initial stanzas with romantic discontent, creating a dialectical irony based upon an affirmation of his social situation and a negation of a mental flight to security. The attitude becomes defiant in subsequent stanzas as he proclaims his liberty, his manhood, and his refusal to bow down before anybody but God. The tone of "My Song" becomes progressively acerbic:

In the middle of my people I am isolated
Because where my cradle was rocked,
With impetus it was cast aside.
A race of pariahs has remained
And to that race I belong.

And we do not have even a homeland, which if it exists
From its bosom knew how to prohibit us;
The burdens may be for the sad man:
And if we have only one right
It has to be the right to die.

Dying for the homeland and enough!
Which is an illegitimate, irrational entity:
For a mulatto of stained caste,
For a vile nigger of a different makeup
Give me a chain and a noose!

That the people tells us day after day
Spilling in our breast bitter bile:
Infamous and servile race, Jewish race,
Don't take another step; this is my land:
Work it in my favor, vile Israel!

And in school, in the street, wherever
And even in the temple where one worships God,
Our children are the first laughingstock
And our mothers await sarcasm
And the insult and the jokes aimed at both!

And to see that wickedness any child cries
Oh profound indignation grips me,
That if I'm black I weave a crown,
That if in my face one does not see the blood
My brow is pure as is my heart.

Pure because my race will not insult
Whom the work of God forms as its equal;
Because my race did not spit in the face
Of a race raised in brotherhood
And it is neither the race of Cain nor criminal.

Ah! if you have such a small soul
If yours is such an ignoble stupidity,
If thus you have a strong reason
And believe that looking at us scorns you
You give pity and grief at the same time.

(En medio de mi pueblo estoy aislado
Porque donde mi cuna se meció,
Con ímpetu arrojada de su lado
Una raza de parias ha quedado
Y a aquesa raza pertenezco yo.

Y ni patria tenemos, que si existe
De su seno nos supo conscribir;
Las cargas sean para el hombre triste:
Y si un solo derecho nos asiste
Ha de scr el derecho de morir.

¡De morir solo por la patria y basta!
Que es un ente bastardo, irracional:
Para un mulato de manchada casta,
Para un vil negro de distinta pasta
¡Una cadena dadme y un dogal!

Eso el pueblo nos dice día a día
Derramando en el seno amarga hiel;
Raza infame y servil, raza judía,
No des un paso más; la tierra es mía:
¡Trabájala en mi pro, vil Israel!

Y en la escuela, en la calle, donde quiera
Y aun en el templo do se adora a Dios,
Son nuestras hijas la irrisión primera
Y a nuestras madres el sarcasmo espera
Y el insulto y las burlas a las dos!

Y al ver esta maldad llora cual niño
O me coje profunda indignación,
Que si soy negro una corona ciño,
Que si en mi frente no se ve el armiño
Pura mi frente está y mi corazón.

Pura porque mi raza no insultará
A quien obra de Dios forma su igual;
Porque mi raza no escupió la cara
De una raza que hermana se criara
Y no es raza Caín ni criminal.

¡Ah! si tenéis el alma tan pequeña
Si es vuestra tan innoble estupidez,
Si así tenéis una razón de peña
Y créis que aún el mirarnos os desdeña
Lástima y aflicción dais a la vez.) (*HM*, 61–63)

The poet's sense of inner exile and displacement is based upon concerns that vary from the so-called Hamitic biblical origins of the *negro* and subsequent condemnation as perpetual Other to discriminatory practices in Argentine society. His repetition of the idea of the black as exile is cloaked in religious metaphors that fail to soften his sense of social estrangement and his affirmation of the dignity of himself and his people. "My Song" ends on a note of hope, though, as the poetic voice views the human race united under a higher authority.

In both *First Verses* and *Hours of Meditation,* Horacio Mendizábal conforms to many of the tenets of romanticism such as creative diversity and a rebellious spirit. At the same time, he never loses sight of the fact that literature can be an important arm in the struggle for black liberation. Black romantics in Argentina upped the ante in the equation by foregrounding the issues of color and discrimination.

Both Elejalde and Mendizábal wrote during the second stage of the postcolonial era as "outcasts." Their thematic concerns embrace the collective and individual struggle toward independence, the questioning of the domination of the majority culture, as well as the recurrent theme of inner exile. As mentioned in the introduction, the postcolonial situation for blacks was different in Argentina than it was in the Caribbean because of a number of factors. Kamau Brathwaite's theory of creolization, for instance, takes into account the relationship between ethnicity and ancestry in confronting postcolonial societies in countries where slavery, repression, and the inability to transcend the position of being the perpetual Other exists. Afro-Argentines were never successful in creating that sense of a homeland and their own literary tradition. The argument of national identity first and the individual afterward was effective in destroying Afro-Argentine continuity while Germans, Italians, and British progressed with their identities intact. The cross-cultural time-space dynamic that undergirds Brathwaite's theory of creolization was not a factor for Afro-Argentine romantic writers precisely because they never forged that unique relationship to place.

CHAPTER TWO
Casildo G. Thompson and
the Failure of *Negritud*

Casildo G. Thompson

In his chapter segment devoted to "Literature: The Artist as Exile," George Reid Andrews makes the following observations concerning Casildo G. Thompson:

> Thompson was the only author who showed any sensitivity toward racial themes. His "Song of Africa," an evocation of the cruelties of the slave trade, employs a striking reversal of traditional porteño racial stereotypes. Here the white man is the savage, "a slavering wild beast" who destroys black families and lives in his relentless greed for profits. Black people are pariahs, as in "My Song,"—Mendizábal—but they are also members of a noble and distinguished race . . . Thus Thompson sounded the trumpet of black pride, a call seldom heard in Buenos Aires.[1]

The attitudes of black writers in nineteenth-century Argentina approximate the ideology of what today would be known as Afrocentrism, or at least *negritud* (négritude), an attitude characteristic of postcolonial discourse. In a recent discussion of the topic, Julio Finn states:

> *Négritude* has been inextricably involved in a long, give-no-quarter war with colonialism and racism. And it is this which makes *Négritude* unique: it is the only artistic movement of modern times whose expressed creed is to redeem the spiritual and cultural values of a people. Born in the red-hot crucible of colonialism its political stance

1. Andrews, *The Afro-Argentines of Buenos Aires,* 175.

51

is as important to it as its artistic one. On the cultural level, *Négritude* vaunts the inimitability of Black civilization; on the human level, it proclaims the innate dignity and beauty of the race—the right of Black peoples proudly to cast their shadows in the sunlight.[2]

One of the basic arguments against *negritud* theory as pointed out in *The Empire Writes Back* is "that its structure is derivative and replicatory, asserting not its difference, as it would claim, but rather its dependence on the categories and features of the colonizing culture." Dependence on the dominant culture is a reality that cannot be denied in most colonial situations and, to a degree, Afro-Argentine literary conventions are derivative. But there is an oppositional stance taken by Thompson in "Song to Africa" ("Song of Africa") aimed at liberating Afro-Argentines through metaphorical escape. The external edifice of this poem is that of the dominant culture, but the essence of "Song to Africa" entails redeeming the "cultural and spiritual values" of black people. As negritudinist expression, "Song to Africa" is an overt condemnation of colonialism and racism. Although Thompson's poem was written in the nineteenth century and does not form part of a *negritud* movement per se, it is a major component in the ongoing black struggle for dignity and self-determination, and not an isolated cry in the wilderness. As a society in transition from foreign domination to one in search of its roots, Argentina kept blacks at a distance, marginalized, a situation that was unacceptable to those who gave so much to the society.

"Song to Africa," first published in 1877, is one of the most overt indictments of racism by an Afro-Argentine poet. As such, it challenges colonial domination and the creation of the negative, black Other. But Thompson is certainly not the only black writer to demonstrate an awareness of the collective origin and presence of this ethnic group as demonstrated throughout this study. He successfully inverts the image of the savage African in a manner that condemns the European and questions his humanity. Thompson evokes an Africa that is a spiritual sanctuary from the inhumane treatment encountered historically by

2. Julio Finn, *Voices of Négritude*, Preface.

Afro-Argentines. This poem is but a small manifestation of the type of redemption the poet seeks, an issue raised in the call by Mateo Elejalde and foregrounded in the works of Horacio Mendizábal.

The image projected by Thompson resonates in the black *payadores* who also view that continent as composed of worry-free societies where blacks are not at the mercy of whites. Thompson, along with the other Afro-Argentine writers of his time, participated in an anti-racist ethnic discourse formulated to alleviate some of the oppression inherent in the society. The rebellious attitude inherent in "Song to Africa" is representative of the romantic mode that stressed freedom and individualism. In the case of Thompson, the thrust is for collective, rather than personal, liberty.

In "Song to Africa," which was perhaps the most well-known Afro-Argentine poem, Thompson poeticizes some of the social concerns of blacks in Argentina in the transition from slavery to representative government. This piece is an attempt to relate the past, present, and future experiences of this population. The militant tone of "Song to Africa" is not surprising, considering the social environment from which it emerges. Portions of this poem first appeared in print in 1877 in *La Juventud* but its definitive version was published by Jorge Miguel Ford in *Outstanding Members of My Race*.[3] This text will be used in my analysis.

"Song to Africa" is in the tradition of contemporary and traditional Afro-Hispanic poetry in that the four key concepts of dualism, identity, liberation, and confrontation provide its thematic basis. This poem begins with a vision of a mythic, paradisiacal Africa that is destroyed by European colonial intervention. The paradoxical vision is presented in the following manner with the first poetic segment:

> Under a radiant sky
> Of clear color, with white clouds
> With woven wings of cherubs,
> A sky with a million stars

---

3. Ford, *Beneméritos*, 113–17. See also Manuel Posadas, "Las poesías del Joven Thompson," 3; Marcos de Estrada, *Argentinos de origen africano*, 135–40; Ildefonso Pereda Valdés, *Antología de la poesía negra americana*, 95–100.

That take refuge in a night of fascination
With a lover's persistence
Caressing the earth with its kiss.
Underneath a sun of flaming colors
Which illuminates space with golden rays:
With an air of scents and a treasury
In rubies and pearls of its flowers:
There is a virgin land that was birthplace
For pain or for fortune
Of a race which is martyr through its history,
A race worthy of glory
Because it is noble and proud
Like the lion who enters the jungle dwelling.
And who in the bitter hour
Dragged it to the abyss of infamy.
Ah! without trembling the fratricidal hand
Of a barbarous, cruel, inhumane Cain . . .

(Bajo un cielo fulgente
De límpido color, con blancas nubes
Como tejidas alas de querubes,
Cielo con millones de luceros
Que refulgen en noche de embeleso
Con amante porfía
Cariciando la tierra con su beso.
Bajo un sol de flamígeros colores
Que ilumina el espacio en rayos de oro:
Con un aire de aromas y un tesoro
En rubíes y perlas de sus flores:
Hay una tierra virgen que fue cuna
Por duelo o por fortuna
De una raza que es mártir por su historia,
Raza digna de gloria
Porque es noble y altiva
Como el león que entre la selva mora.
Y que en acerba hora
Arrastróla al abismo de la infamia.
¡Ah! sin temblar la fratricida mano
De un bárbaro Caín, cruel, inhumano . . .)

The initial metaphoric environment is of harmony between humans and their surroundings, built on a romantic scaffolding of paradise lost. Martyrdom and oppression are the destructive forces that have had such a devastating impact upon an entire ethnic group whose plight the poet relates to biblical myths. This poem is a classic example of the *rhetorical* mode of African literature as conceptualized by Edward Kamau Brathwaite. In this category, "The writer uses Africa as mask, signal of *nomen*. He doesn't know very much about Africa necessarily, although he reflects a deep desire to make connection. But he is only saying the word 'Africa' or invoking a dream of the Congo, Senegal, Niger, the Zulu, Nile or Zambesi. He is not necessarily celebrating or activating the African presence."[4]

The rhetorical question is then employed to evoke a positive image of Africa and an answer regarding the victims of the negative process of imprisonment and oppression:

> Do you know the name of
> That divine and blessed land
> That jewel which God bequeathed to the world,
> That chaste offended virgin
> Of humiliated prominence?
> Its name is AFRICA, listen, beautiful Africa!
> It is the birthplace of the Black: it is the homeland
> Of the eternal exile who weeps for it
> And far from his home
> Lifts up in a strange land his sonorous voice
> Singing the song of his sorrows.
> That is the cradle of the Black,
> Of the universal pariah . . . The blazing sun
> Which kissed your proud face in childhood
> Also saw you leave in sad pain.
> With bloodied feet
> Dragging the shackle, looking at the sky,
> A witness to your shame and the vile brand
> The ferocious hangman put on your neck.
> That land, the seductive image

4. Edward Kamau Brathwaite, *Roots,* 211.

Of a lost paradise of delights,
Cloaked itself in mourning, from the dawn
To the death of the sun of many centuries.
Her beautiful riverbanks
That swift ships populated yesterday,
Her smiling and flowery shores,
Her forests and her jungles, fell ill
Held a wake for her . . .

(¿Sabéis cómo se llama
Esa tierra divina y bendecida,
Esa joya que al mundo Dios legara,
Esa púdica virgen ofendida
Que humillada descuella?
Se llama AFRICA, oíd, Africa bella!
Es la cuna del negro: ésa es la patria
Del eterno proscripto que la llora
Y lejos de sus lares
Eleva en tierra extraña voz sonora
Entonando el cantar de los pesares.
Del negro ésa es la cuna,
Del paria universal . . . El sol ardiente
Que besó en la niñez su altiva frente
También le vio partir con triste duelo.
Con planta ensangrentada
Arrastrando el dogal, mirando al cielo,
Testigo de su afrenta y del vil sello
Que un verdugo feroz le puso al cuello.
Esa tierra, la imagen seductora
De un perdido paraíso de delicias,
De luto se cubrió, desde la aurora
Al ocaso del sol de muchos siglos.
Sus hermosas riberas
Que poblaron ayer barcas ligeras,
Sus márgenes risueñas y floridas,
Sus bosques y sus selvas, adolidas
Veláronse la *face*. . .

Africa, the matrix, the womb of black civilization, a safe haven for
a maligned ethnic group, is characterized by positive imagery, as if it

were the chosen land. The illusion of peace and serenity is interrupted by the harsh realities of the slave trade. Africa is likened to a maiden being violated by a lecherous beast. The archetypal abode, symbolized by classical images of peace, tranquility, and harmony in the human and natural orders, are interrupted by the brutal insensitivities of the flesh traffic.

Africa is portrayed as being in harmony with the celestial order through anaphora with "esa," which prefaces imagery of a God-given state of being. It was not destined to become a source of cheap labor for the exploiters. The poetic voice views the subsequent ramifications upon the continent and its inhabitants in existential terms, couched in the language of alienation, estrangement, psychological marginalization, and perpetual otherness. The dichotomy is drawn between the "lost paradise of delights" and a space covered by the "death of the sun of many centuries."

The image of Africa projected in this poem is one of a poet familiar with the continent on a rhetorical level. Africa does not transcend the status of *nomen,* of psychological refuge for blacks subjected to intolerable conditions in Argentina. Slavery and its ramifications are phenomena that changed an imagined peaceful civilization in charge of its own destiny into a producer of some of the most exploited commodities in history:

> Do you know what happens and why sadly
> The beautiful African virgin
> Takes off her fine clothes
> And does not wear the smile of a sultan?
> Because an hour sounded, a wretched hour!
> Of revulsion and shame when one shout
> Which said *slavery* was heard everywhere
> And from the hushed valley to the agitated sea,
> From the tall peak to the low forest
> A lecherous beast
> Named the white man
> Ripped the breast of virgin Africa
> With brutal greediness, bloody fury.
> Beginning with that day
> Of tears and pain

The rays in the sky did not shine
From the sun of justice.
The trunk of the *baobab* which was the house
Of a hundred generations
A home which generous nature gave
And respected tigers and lions
Of the African jungle
Fell to the blow of the hangman's axe
And because he did this
Amid screams the boy and maiden left
With colored lips and fiery eyes
With a sparkling look and prayerful voice,
And a universal outcry was heard in the air
Which pierced the clouds and arrived in heaven
Demanding pity for that land;
Heaven was deaf
Not even the shout of the innocent child
Which found an echo in every human breast
Found the heart of the white man merciful.
The eloquent prayer
That maternal lips mumbled
Heard cold, insensible, the homicide:
That human beast
Wished that the weak child
In the blessed arms of its mother
Suffer the blows of his whip.

(¿Sabéis lo que sucede y por qué triste
La bellísima virgen africana
Sus galas se desviste
Y no ostenta sonrisa de sultana?
Porque sonó una hora ¡hora maldita!
De oprobio y de vergüenza en que una grita
Que dijo ¡*esclavitud!* se oyó en los aires,
Y del callado valle al mar airado,
Desde la altiva cumbre al bajo prado
Una fiera sedienta
Que se llamó hombre blanco,
El seno desgarró al Africa virgen
Con avidez brutal, saña sangrienta.

A contar de aquel día
De lágrimas y duelo
No brillaron los rayos en el cielo
Del sol de la justicia.
El tronco del *baobab* que fue la choza
De cien generaciones,
Hogar que dio natura generosa
Y respetaron tigres y leones
De la africana selva,
Cayó al golpe del hacha del verdugo
Y porque asía éste plugo
Entre ¡ayes! salió el niño y la doncella
De labios de color y ojos de fuego
De chispeante mirar y voz de ruego,
Y universal clamor se oyó en los aires
Que atravesó la nube y llegó al cielo
Demandando piedad para aquel suelo;
El cielo estaba sordo,
Ni aun el grito del párvulo inocente
Que en todo pecho humano encuentra eco
El corazón del blanco halló clemente.
La plegaria sentida
Que los maternos labios balbucearan
Oyó frío, insensible, el homicida:
Aquella humana fiera
Quiso que el débil niño
En los benditos brazos de su madre
Los golpes de su látigo sufriera.)

The slaver is equated with the hangman/executioner who, ironically, has support from the natural order. Black appeals for justice and pity go unheeded in a system where no age distinction is made among the exploited. The brutality of shameful slavery is driven home by the poet through images of blood, tears, chains, whips, and innocent children being ripped from their parents' arms.

Africa personified stands in stark juxtaposition to the inhumane acts of savagery committed against its people by the intruders. The contrast between the physical environment and human behavior remains constant throughout the poem. Nature represents all that is good while human beings are portrayed as destructive forces. The *baobab* tree, indigenous to Africa and India, serves as a positive identity marker within this context of exploitation and genocide.

In spite of its romantic artifice, "Song to Africa" is a serious assessment of important aspects of the black experience. The atrocities committed in Africa are resumed in Argentina, where the destruction of black institutions continues:

> Ah, despot and cruel; he is the owner
> Who grants life and hands out death,
> Who does not know the law, neither strong nor weak,
> Nor that righteous God,
> Thus the black man saw him arrive
> In the secular doorway of his dwelling,
> Eternal sanctuary of pleasant happiness
> Profaned by no one.
> And to look at the white man before him threatening,
> With iron in his right hand,
> He bows submissively
> Pretending to calm his sinister rage.
> He then lifts his voice in a sweet plea
> While screams of fire shoot through his face
> Which would perhaps move even the beasts.
> "Halt"—the black man says—"this is the hut
> Which shelters the memory of a wife
> Who permeated my life with love
> And was the light of my eyes
> Whose shine will be extinguished in my agony.
> Stop for mercy! Here were born
> Two pieces of my soul
> Who submerged me in blessed calm;
> Two stars, two pearls, my two children,
> Precious talismans
> Who gave vigor to my humbled strength
> And in their abundance of love infused me with life."
>
> But the inhuman white man
> Grinning with contempt, advances his step
> "Halt"—the black man implores—"let your foot

Respect the humble temple of my happiness."
And the inexorable white man,
Lashing the brave face of the black man,
Says to him with intolerable disdain:
"Step aside vile nigger! Step aside slave! . . ."
Aye cursed, cursed a thousand times
May you be white man without faith, may your cruel memory
Be an eternal curse for your history
Let it dishonor the children of your children
And let them wear it on their faces.
The stain of infamy that you made
Which the black man wears eternally
The wounds of his soul that you opened up.
May you be cursed, yes, until you are thrown
From the bosom of the earth,
Because you were an abortion
A sign of crass and fratricidal war.

(Ah! déspota y cruel; él es el amo
Que concede la vida y da la muerte,
Que no conoce ley, débil ni fuerte,
Ni aquel Dios justiciero,
Así lo vio llegar el hombre negro
Al dintel secular de su morada,
Santuario eterno de tranquila dicha
Por nadie profanada.
Y al mirarle ante sí amenazante
Con el hierro en la diestra,
Se inclina suplicante
Pretendiendo calmar su ira siniestra.
Eleva pues la voz con dulce ruego
Mientras surca su faz llanto de fuego
Que conmoviera acaso hasta las fieras.
"Detente"—el negro dice—"ésta es la choza
Do se anida el recuerdo de una esposa
Que perfumó de amor la vida mía
Y fue luz de mis ojos
Que extinguirá su brillo en mi agonía.
Detente por piedad! aquí nacieron
Dos trozos de mi alma

Que me inundaron en bendita calma;
Dos estrellas, dos perlas, mis dos hijos,
Preciosos talismanes
Que dan nervio a mi fuerza ya abatida
Y en su raudal de amor me infunden vida."

Pero el blanco inhumano
Sonriendo con desprecio, el pie adelanta:
"Detente—el negro implora—que tu planta
Respete el templo humilde de mi dicha."
Y el blanco inexorable,
Fustigando del negro el rostro bravo,
Le dice con desdén intolerable:
"Aparta negro vil! aparta esclavo! . . ."
Ah! maldito, maldito por mil veces
Seas blanco sin fe, tu cruel memoria
Sea eterno baldón para tu historia
Que deshonre a los hijos de tus hijos
Y lleven en la frente
La mancha de la infamia que tu hicieras
Cual lleva el hombre negro eternamente
Las heridas del alma que le abrieras.
Maldito seas, sí, que hasta te arroje
De su seno la tierra,
Porque fuiste su aborto
Signo de cruda y fratricida guerra.)

The white still maintains life-and-death control over the black and seems to have supplanted God in determining their destiny in Argentina during this period. Not even the black home and family are immune to indiscriminate incursions by the white master, who in slavery is characterized as inhuman, cruel, and disrespectful. From Africa to Argentina, there has been a process of degradation of blacks through capture, imprisonment, and enslavement. "Song to Africa" is Casildo Thompson's attempt to portray the reality of victimized Afro-Argentines who are estranged and powerless.

The reaction of the black in this situation is paradoxical, a mixture of accommodation and rage: "Pretending to calm his irate hostility / he raises his voice with a sweet plea / while a scream of fire covers his face / that would move even beasts." The black man's plea to save his family, based upon values such as love, stability, and unity, are ignored. "Step aside vile *negro!* Step aside slave." The reply is significant because the image of slavery is one that Afro-Argentines were unable to discard during their centuries of existence in that country. The black's rage in "Song to Africa," which he is unable to transform to actions due to possible reprisals and punishment, is insufficient to alleviate the dehumanizing circumstances with which he is confronted.

There is an abrupt ideological shift by the poet, who states that in spite of his rage, his task is to promote harmony and to address more esoteric issues:

> But, the rage does not cease.
> The poet does not achieve his mission
> Of hate in the region, and of his lyre
> Only its chord is sweet and melodious
> If the olive branch symbolizes peace
> And love is the deity
> Where one goes to drink divine inspiration,
> Let any voice of a wandering siren
> Bring beings in a strange world
> To the region of light where hate ceases
> And the dawn of brotherhood begins.

> (Mas, no cesa la ira.
> Su misión el poeta no realiza
> Del odio en la región, y de su lira
> Solo es dulce el acorde y melodioso
> Si de la paz la oliva simboliza
> Y es el amor el numen
> Do va a beber la inspiración divina,
> Que cual voz de sirena peregrina
> Traiga a los seres en el mundo extraños
> A la región de luz do el odio cesa
> Y de fraternidad la aurora empieza.)

In spite of the pain and suffering, blacks are miraculously supposed to forgive and forget. Herein lies the central irony of "Song to Africa." In spite of surface appearances, neither victim nor victimizer is capable of erasing the historical past. The image of blacks as objects of the colonial process persists to this day. Romantic poets, however, are eternal optimists:

> There are brilliant clouds in the sky:
> A splendid dawn appears
> Among mists of pearl and rose
> Foreshadowing a radiant and new day,
> A harmony is felt in space
> Whose celestial echo enraptures the soul
> In divine ecstasy;
> So sweet is my rumor, so beautiful.
> The jungle shudders, the sea sighs;
> And in those waves of crystal and snow.
> The blue sky looks at itself
> As a pleased woman in a polished mirror.
> From the flowers of virgin meadows
> To the sob of trembling breezes
> Of drunken aroma
> Swift waves surge . . .
> Do you know what happens?
> Do you know why impassioned nature
> Discovers the treasure where it is sheltered?
> Because the sun which Africa awaits arrives:
> A sun which to the oppressed and the slave
> A voice of prophecy predicted,
> The sun of Redemption: the hour sounded
> In the quadrant of destiny
> Now in the name of love slaves and tyrants
> Shake hands
> Thus the Equality of Justice joins
> Them in a confused embrace.
>
> (Hay en el cielo nubes de oriflama:
> Aparece una aurora esplendorosa
> Entre velos de nácar y de rosa
> Presagiando un radiante y nuevo día,
> Se siente en el espacio una armonía
> Cuyo eco celestial arroba el alma
> En éxtasis divino;

Tan dulce es mi rumor, tan peregrino.
La selva se estremece, el mar suspira;
Y en esas ondas de cristal y nieve
El cielo azul se mira
Como mujer a gusto en terso espejo.
De las flores de vírgenes praderas
Al sollozo del aura estremecidas
De embriagador aroma
Surgen olas ligeras . . .
¿Sabéis lo que sucede?
¿Sabéis por qué natura conmovida
El tesoro descubre do se anida?
Porque viene ya el sol que Africa espera:
El sol que al oprimido y al esclavo
Una voz de profeta predijera,
El sol de Redención: sonó la hora
En la cuadrante del destino
Ya en nombre del amor se dan las manos
Esclavos y tiranos
Pues la Igualdad de la Justicia hermana
Los quiere en un abrazo confundidos.)

The poet's final demand is for equality and justice, since the legacy of slavery remains a central issue in the Afro-Argentine experience. Contempt and humiliation, as pointed out in *La Broma,* are two social attitudes they have not been able to overcome, in spite of the new day that the poet sees on the horizon. The final verses of "Song to Africa" are ambivalent and suggestive, despite the rhetoric of harmony, of an eternal conflict between black and white in Argentina.

In the final stanzas of "Song to Africa," the poet's stance regarding the relationship between aesthetics and the social function of his verse is very similar to the position taken by Mendizábal. Poetry should be used to articulate the frustrations felt by blacks as well as their social concerns, but it should also be a vehicle to promote harmony between blacks and whites in Argentina. This peaceful coexistence will be achieved only if Afro-Argentines receive equal and just treatment, which is not likely to occur because of the structure of power in society.

In the final analysis, though, Thompson seeks redemption for blacks who have been oppressed and enslaved but must now take the initiative in forging ethnic harmony. "Song to Africa" is structured around the dialectical tension between the aggressive white (ferocious hangman, lecherous beast, inhumane white) and the victimized black (martyr race, worthy of glory). This poem articulates in verse some of the same attitudes evident in Afro-Argentine periodicals such as *La Juventud* and *La Broma.* "Song to Africa" represents a persuasive contribution to the development of an Afro-Argentine discourse against oppression and for liberation. Thompson's Africa is rhetorical rather than real, and as stated presents this continent as a *nomen,* an idea that the poet does not comprehend fully. Africa remains a part of the poet's collective memory but he does not go so far as to try to write "literature of reconnection" or of "African expression," which would involve the incorporation of symbols and linguistic norms associated with Africa.

Although this poem has been perceived as unique ever since it first began circulating in 1877, the first real analysis of this work is by Manuel T. Posadas, who presents a balanced view of the author and his work because

> We don't believe that young Thompson is a luminous constellation who appears amongst us to show us the road to redemption, nor a stellar figure who may be permitted to occupy first place among those who, esteemed for their talent and through their compositions have shown us their profound literary knowledge but if he is our intimate connection, who is a fresh and robust intelligence, whose more than four fine versifications will have his signature, on some brilliant compositions.
>
> But since Thompson reveals himself a true poet filled with inspiration and with life, through his facility of language, the greatness of concepts, the elegance of style and which the ear less attuned to poetry perceives that the verse has flowed spontaneously and the poet has not hunted for consonants nor has he seemed rushed by metrics, . . .
>
> If it is true that these verses will bring to the memory of those who suffered such cruel humiliation the sad and painful memory of its injustice as a barbarous martyrdom, it is also true that those of us who descend from that virile race, feel too strongly against them to curse a thousand times and sing about liberty at others.

The outcome would have been much happier if it ended with the suicide of the black man caused by the desperation of not being able to stop the entrance into his hut by the white man or death to the latter at the hands of the former.[5]

Posadas recognizes that Thompson has used poetry as an instrument to raise the level of social awareness. However, Posadas questions both the actions of the black protagonist of "Song to Africa" and the relevance of its message to Afro-Argentines. He is as ambivalent as Thompson when he states: "it is true also that those of us who descend from this virile race, feel too strongly for them to bad mouth tyranny a thousand times and sing a few other times to liberty." In the end, both Thompson and Posadas are seeking an accommodation as social equals.

As a manifestation of postcolonial expression, "Song to Africa" exemplifies basic historical realities—"subjugation, domination, diaspora, displacement"—that Afro-Argentines resisted in order to survive. The poem is structured in a fashion that underscores crucial moments of crisis and remains a testimonial to the indomitable spirit of Afro-Argentines.

Thompson's other poem that has survived to the present is entitled, "En la muerte de la niña María Tránsito Quiroga" (On the death of the child María Tránsito Quiroga):

> Fly away dove, fly away, this is not your nest
> The jail that is this world; away from its mire,
> Your white wings fleeing with speed,
> Search for a nest in heaven, there there is no pain!
>   Here on this earth
>   A tomb remains
> Which upon pointing out the furrow of your step,
> Shows a trail of tears and flowers.
>
> Fly away dove, fly away; you wanted
> To be white virginal snow of the mountain
> And did not wait for the sun, you fled swiftly
> At early daybreak.

5. Posadas, "Las poesías del joven Thompson," 1–2.

For that reason you put on a
   White tiara
And roses and lilies argue
Who is to adorn you, the most chaste.

It seems like destiny, there in your cradle,
Would give to your life symbolism in your name,
Well they called you Tránsito in the world
Being so brief and transitory your stay
    But in the eternal
    Mansion of pleasure
What limit can your life find
If you are the jewel which adorns God's throne?

Fly away, white dove, fly away, fly away;
Upon the black clouds of space
Already hang your innocent wings
And the sun of adventure illuminates you:
    Beneath those clouds
    Upon this plain,
Others await the hour of rest
And the radiance of eternal stars . . .
You who reside with God, pray, dove
For those who await the day of happiness.

(Vuela paloma, vuela, no es tu nido
La cárcel de este mundo; de su lodo,
Tus blancas alas con presteza huyendo,
Buscan nido en el cielo, allá no hay dolor!
    Aquí en la tierra
    Queda una loza
Que al señalar el zurco de tu paso,
Muestra huella de lágrimas y flores.

Vuela paloma, vuela; tu quisiste
Ser nieve virginal de la montaña
Y no esperaste al sol, huiste ligera
Cuando recien se despertaba el alba.
    Por eso ciñes
    Diadema blanca,

Y rosas y azucenas se disputan
Quien es, para adornarte, la más casta.

Parece que el destino, allá en tu cuna,
Diera a tu vida símbolo en tu nombre,
Pues te llamaste Tránsito en el mundo
Siendo breve tu estancia y transitoria
    Pero en la eterna
    Mansión del gozo
¿Qué límite encontrar puede tu vida
Si eres joya que a Dios adorna el trono?

Vuela, paloma blanca, vuela, vuela;
Sobre las nubes negras del espacio
Se ciernen ya tus alas inocentes
Y te ilumina sol de venturanza:
    Bajo esas nubes,
    Sobre este páramo,
Otros esperan la hora del reposo
Y el fulgar de los astros eternales . . .
Tú que moras con Dios, ruega, paloma.
Por los que el día de la dicha aguardan.)[6]

Literally, "On the Death of the Child María Tránsito Quiroga" is a eulogy attesting to the innocence and purity of its protagonist as symbolized by the dominant imagery of whiteness. Symbolically, however, the theme of escape from oppressive conditions is analogous to the Afro-Argentine condition. This poem is structured around images of movement, of flight, of transition from the physical world to the spiritual. At the poem's core is the dichotomy between life and death, between black and white, between the concrete and the ineffable. The color white, associated with death in conjunction with other funeral images, is presented in such a way as to soften the impact of personal loss. Beginning in the initial stanza, the world-as-jail image is built upon with a great deal of anxiety. Given the attitude of Thompson and the

6. Casildo G. Thompson, "En la muerte de la niña María Tránsito Quiroga," *La Perla* 1, no. 29 (6 de octubre 1878): 3.

double voicedness of Afro-Argentine writers of this era, could not the desire for a better life "For those who await the day of happiness" be wishful thinking to alleviate the plight of the entire black population? This poem appears to be about a lot more than innocent death if we associate the "black clouds" with the burdens of Afro-Argentine existence.

Jorge Miguel Ford

The idea of moving from the individual to the collective black experience was given serious treatment by Jorge Miguel Ford in *Outstanding Members of My Race*. Ford's intention was to raise the consciousness of Argentines in regard to the important roles blacks played in that society. In the introductory essay to this rare book, entitled "La redención de una raza" (The redemption of a race), Augusto Marcó del Pont states:

> This book was written to stimulate the black man, showing him up close examples of merit of his race that exists in this Nation. It will probably not raise much of a storm but the home of the black man will have a book of practical lessons in whose pages he will find enough nourishment to strengthen his spirit. He will discover in those biographies, the souls of his illustrious companions of those black Argentines who, victors in the battles of the arts and on the battlefield, have built with their works their pedestal of glory, to indicate to the rest, from the heights where they tread, the road to follow from today forward. Now they have a constant source of inspiration, the beings who were born with black skin.[7]

Since the accomplishments of Afro-Argentines were not well known to the general public, Ford assumed the responsibility of righting this wrong. Of the fourteen social profiles contained in *Outstanding Members of My Race,* six are devoted to military men (Lorenzo I. Barcala, Domingo Sosa, Felipe Mansilla, Casildo Thompson, Eduardo Magee, José María Morales); two are composers (Federico Espinosa, Zenón Rolón); two are intellectuals (Froilán P. Bello, Casildo G. Thompson);

7. Ford, *Beneméritos,* 5.

one is a philanthropist (Eugenio Sar); one is a scribe (Tomás B. Platero); one is a newspaperman (Manuel G. Posadas); and one is a poet (Horacio Mendizábal). Of these distinguished Afro-Argentines, Eugenio Sar was the founder in 1877 of La Protectora, the mutual aid society, and Froilán P. Bello was the founder in 1884 of *El Eco Artístico,* a literary journal, copies of which cannot be located in Argentina or abroad.

Ford's motivation for penning this one-of-a-kind document is clearly stated: "Thus animated by a genuine feeling of veneration of the tireless workers, the descendants of the African race, those who excelled breaking the routine to which they were subjected, we will not hesitate in attempting to break the overwhelming calm in which the community sways to the breeze of indifference, with our infertile pen."[8] *Outstanding Members of My Race* is conceived as a public service project designed to keep the historic black experience at center stage in Argentina. This book is not an end unto itself, since its author has other plans: "if the public give us the reception we desire, we will not be many months before presenting the second volume of *Outstanding Members of My Race.*" Ford's dream of a second volume was never realized.

It is interesting to note that while Ford the biographer was extremely Afrocentric, Ford the poet was a romantic. This bent is evident in a poem dedicated to "Mariano Moreno," the Argentine leader:

> Lend me, inspiration, your noble courage
> And on the wings of the most noble patriotism
> Permit that in the temple of civilism
> My thought is also discovered.
>
> Mariano Moreno is the strong wind
> Which agitates my country with altruism
> When he wished to climb over egoism
> With his talent to reach sacred liberty.
>
> Champion of progress! It was his idea
> The seed of august democracy
> Which was born for the people of May

8. Ford, *Beneméritos,* 8.

And were the flames of that torch extinguished
By the vortex of the sea? A crass disgrace
But still in the sea his flame burned!

(Préstame, inspiración, tu noble aliento
Y en alas del más noble patriotismo
Permite que en el templo del civismo
Se descubra también mi pensamiento.

Es Mariano Moreno el faudo viento
Que agitara mi patria con altruismo
Cuando ansiaba escalar el egoismo
La sacra libertad con su talento.

¡Adalid del progreso! . . . Fue su idea
La simiente de augusta democracia
Para el pueblo de mayo que nacía

¿Y apagaron las llamas de esa tea
Voragines del mar? . . . Ruda desgracia
Mas aun en el mar su fuego ardía!)[9]

Afro-Argentine poets of this period were caught in a double bind, a no-win situation. If they wanted to be accepted by the majority culture, they had to embrace certain themes that were considered "proper" by those who established literary standards. At the same time, Afro-Argentine writers had to satisfy two constituents within the black community, those who were in tune with mainstream traditions as well as those who insisted that literature must also appeal to the so-called marginal individuals. The contending forces either neutralized black

9. Jorge Miguel Ford, "Mariano Moreno," *El Eco de Flores* 4, no. 115 (9 de julio 1911): 1. Mariano Moreno edited a document in 1809 entitled *Representación de los labradores y hacendados de las campañas de la Banda Oriental y Occidental del Río de la Plata* that was supposed to have had an impact on the subsequent Argentine fight against foreign domination initiated by the Revolution of May 1810. Some historians maintain that Moreno's document had no impact on the Revolution while others present the opposite opinion. Consult, for example, Ramallo, *Historia Argentina fundamental*, 189–90.

artists or forced them to come down on the side of the majority if they wished to remain true to their craft.

The fact that black writers in Argentina refused to be deterred by internal factors attests to their commitment as writers with a social mission. The idea of leaving a written record of their existence in Argentina appeared to be far more important than being popular with the literary elite. Afro-Argentine artists were unanimous in their hope for a society where blacks were not at the mercy of whites. Through their social concerns and modes of expression, these writers participated in an Afro-Argentine discourse formulated to alleviate some of the oppression inherent in society and to place positive emphasis upon the black presence.

Although they did not form a part of an international black literary movement, Thompson and Ford, as well as Elejalde and Mendizábal, were certainly at odds with colonialism and racism. Each of the poets published a work calling for the redemption of the cultural values of Afro-Argentines. As such, they questioned the legitimacy of their marginal status within the postcolonial context. The ability of Casildo G. Thompson and other writers to sustain Afrocentric topics was limited by access to publication outlets, audiences, and a rapidly changing social ideology. Given the fluid nature of Argentine society at the turn of this century, there were many who did not wish to be identified with an African past. Hence the idea of affirming blackness in that particular milieu was not a viable option. *Negritud* was miscegenated out of existence along with the majority of the black population.

CHAPTER THREE

The *Criollista* Spirit or the Black Writer as *Payador*

The alienation and rejection felt by Afro-Argentine writers did not end with romanticism but carried over into the *criollista* period as well. This, too, was an era of nationalistic fervor that witnessed a continuing decline in Afro-Argentine influence. In his assessment of the complex social environment created at the turn of the century between natives and immigrants in Argentina, Adolfo Prieto writes: "Paradoxically, nevertheless, in that air of foreignness and cosmopolitanism, the predominant tone was creole or creolized expression; the plasma which seemed destined to unite the diverse fragments of the racial and cultural mosaic was constituted upon a singular image of the country dweller and his language."[1] The adaptation of Afro-Argentines to *criollo* values is extremely logical, given their historical sense of loyalty and dedication to the *patria.* If the unifying matrix were to be *criollismo,* it is not surprising that they were some of the most fervent supporters of these values. After all, the word *criollo,* in its Latin American context, according to Corominas, is an adaptation of the Portuguese word *crioulo,* which means "the slave born in the house of his master" or "the black born in the colony, to differentiate from the one who comes via the trade." Only later did this term assume its present significance of "a white born in the colonies."[2] As nonindigenous Argentines, blacks had a very important stake in the country's cultural direction. Prieto continues:

1. Adolfo Prieto, *El discurso criollista en la formación de la Argentina moderna,* 18.
2. Joan Corominas, *Diccionario crítico etimológico de la lengua castellana,* 943–44.

For the leading groups of the native population, that creolism could signify the mode of affirmation of their own legitimacy and the method of rejection of the disquieting presence of the foreigner. For the popular sectors of that same native population, displaced from their places of origin and settled in cities that creolism could be an expression of nostalgia or a substitute form of rebellion against the estrangement and the impositions of the urban scene. And for many foreigners it could signify the immediate and visible form of assimilation the credential of citizenship they could invoke to integrate themselves with full rights in the growing torrent of social life.[3]

Although Prieto does not mention the word "Afro-Argentine" or any other euphemisms associated with blackness, these assumptions are on the mark regarding the social situation and the perceptions of this segment of the population. Afro-Argentines were strangers in their own homeland and were certainly trying to affirm their own legitimacy while dealing with the ominous foreign presence.

Afro-Argentine popular poets are eloquent examples of turn-of-the-century manifestations of *criollismo*. Higinio Cazón, Luis García Morel, and Gabino Ezeiza, for example, are recognized as first-rate artist/performers in the long Argentine tradition of oral popular culture. Subsequently, a limited number of their poems have been anthologized and accepted as a part of the national literature. It is as *serious* writers that these poets have not been given due consideration. The majority of their poetry interprets, in culturalist fashion, the country, its inhabitants, customs, and problems. They wrote primarily in the octosyllabic verse form with consonant rhyme, which is in the Hispanic oral tradition.

George Reid Andrews places the black *payadores* and their role in proper perspective when he writes

There was one area of musical endeavor, however, in which the Afro-Argentines remained firmly in control throughout the nineteenth century and well into the twentieth. That is only to be expected, considering that the art form was almost purely African in its derivation.

3. Prieto, *El discurso criollista,* 18–19.

This was the *payada,* a sort of poetic duel in which two guitarist-singers spontaneously composed verses on a given theme or in response to each other's challenges. A vocal variation of the tapadas, the drum duels, the *payada* was the lineal descendant of the African tradition of musical contests of skill, a tradition which has produced similar phenomena in every American country where there is a large black population.[4]

Afro-Argentine poets such as Ezeiza, Cazón, and García Morel learned early on that their careers as "traditional" artists were not very promising. It has been written and often assumed that Ezeiza, for instance, was always a popular poet, a *payador* who earned his living and reputation in oral versification contests. On the contrary, Ezeiza was at one point in his life an exceptional romantic poet and coeditor of *La Juventud,* one of the most stable black periodicals of the nineteenth century in Argentina.

Ezeiza's career was followed very carefully by the rival editors of *La Broma.* On one occasion, they wrote:

> The reader will remember Gabino M. Ezeiza? Gabino is one of the collaborators of *La Juventud,* a newspaper which has lived longer than others lived. Well, Gabino has dedicated himself to the *paya,* he sings magnificently, and not to be funny, we don't dare to say: the man sings more than a goldfinch. For certain, or what we suspect, is that Gabino is paid. The man looks for life; it is not a dishonor, and if we do not know that Gabino is paid, it is because where we have heard him perform many times, is in the joint "Locos Alegres" located on Córdoba Street between Artes and Cerrito. Very well: let Gabino Ezeiza sing; let the action continue![5]

It is not surprising that many Afro-Argentines would turn to the popular entertainment profession of the *payador,* since blacks were often associated with the nonserious, playful aspects of the genre, as is evident, for instance, in *Martin Fierro,* the popular gaucho epic by José Hernández. The root word *payo* means "aldeano," "pastor,"

4. Andrews, *The Afro-Argentines of Buenos Aires,* 170.
5. *La Broma* 2, no. 55 (enero 1882): 3.

"rústico," with the obvious connotation of country bumpkin. *Paya,* another derivation, means "bobona," "tonta," "persona inculta," "inútil." *Payada, payador,* and *payaso* (clown) are from the same root.[6]

Although Afro-Argentine *payadores* were the best in their profession, the majority of them died poor because of personal habits and the exigencies of the profession. As in Argentine society, black artists were treated differently from their counterparts. It was not uncommon for slurs and insults relating to color to be a part of the performance. For example, García Morel, described by Ismael Moya as "recio criollo de señalada progenie africana" ("a strong creole of pronounced African lineage"), recalls his renowned *payada* with Ramón Vieytes: "He believed I was an easy enemy. And since I made him work he tried to dazzle me with a series of offensive verses which alluded to the color of my skin, my nappy hair, my lisp. This made some laugh and upset others."[7] Moya goes on to relate the classic affront of Maximiliano Santillán to Ezeiza before their *payada,* which also carried racist overtones, regardless of whether the intent was comic or serious:

> Where is that black poet
> who has such a reputation?
> Tell him that Santillán
> does not respect any nigger.

> (¿Dónde está ese negro poeta
> que tanta fama le dan?
> Díganle que Santillán
> a ningún negro respeta.)

To excel in their profession, García Morel, Ezeiza, and Cazón had to overcome obstacles of color and money, but they left behind a proud legacy that deserves to be recognized.

Gabino Ezeiza is the author of numerous poetry chapbooks. Many of his poems are contained in seven volumes that will be discussed in this chapter. Higinio D. Cazón is the author of *Alegrías y pesares: canciones*

---

6. Corominas, *Diccionario crítico etimológico,* 3, 701.
7. Ismael Moya, *El arte de los payadores,* 306.

nacionales (Joys and sorrows: national songs, n.d.), while Luis García Morel published *Gauchesco* (n.d.) and *Esquinas líricas (versos)* (Lyric corners [verses], 1937). The majority of these poems reflect *criollista* concerns—the country, its inhabitants, customs, problems, that is, Argentine culture. This discussion will treat relevant works by Cazón, García Morel, and Ezeiza in this order, with Ezeiza presented as the maximum expression of the Afro-Argentine *payador.*

Higinio Cazón

Joys and Sorrows: National Songs consists of poems written by and dedicated to Higinio Cazón and others dedicated to him by friends. The majority of the selections are *criollista* in tone, interpreting Argentine culture. Written between 1889 and 1909, *Alegrías y pesares* contains widely distributed poems such as "El ombú coposo" (The bushy ombú), "El Gaucho" (The Gaucho), and "Recuerdos históricos: Tucumán y Salta" (Historical memories: Tucumán and Salta), as well as other selections.

Narrated in popular, octosyllabic verse from the perspective of the poet/witness, "The Bushy Ombú" is a tale of double suicide beneath the legendary solitude of the *ombú* tree. The environment is dreamlike/surreal, in which an anticipated intense romantic encounter ends in tragedy when a sleeping lover is mistaken for dead. In the second stanza, the poet/spy narrates:

> Upon seeing him I was surprised
> But I said: he must be crazy!
> I saw him wipe his brow
> Even threw off his hat
> Gritted his teeth
> Then began immediately
> That disgraceful mistake
> For me he found rest
> While napping
> Under the bushy *ombú.*
>
> (Al verlo quedé admirado
> Mas dije: ¡será demente!

Lo vi secarse la frente
Hasta el sombrero tirar
Sus dientes a rechinar
Comenzaron al instante
Aquel desgraciado errante
Para mi encontró reposo
Al quedarse dormitando
Bajo de un ombú coposo.)[8]

The poet employs irony, verbal and situational, to create a scene in which ignorance and a misinterpretation of the circumstances lead to irrational behavior by the female protagonist:

A little knife inlaid
With emerald she had,
In her hand it glowed
Pointed toward her heart
She sat down at his side
Controlled her sobs
With the greatest cold blood
Plunged it in her beautiful breast
Fell half agonizing.
Beneath the bushy *ombú*.

(Un puñalito incrustado
Con esmeralda tenía,
En su mano relucía
Inclinado al corazón
Al lado de él sentó
Sus sollozos reprimía
Con la mayor sangre fría

8. Higinio Cazón, *Alegrías y pesares: canciones nacionales*, 45–46. Subsequent references will appear in the text as *AP.* Nestor Ortiz Oderigo lists two additional works published by Cazón that I have not been able to find. They are *El gaucho de las sierras* and *Horas amargas* in *Aspectos de la cultura africana en el Río de la Plata*, 189. This poem parallels the legend of Pyramus and Thisbe, two famous lovers of Babylon who were united in death. Pyramus killed himself with a sword when he saw blood that he mistakenly believed belonged to Thisbe. She, in turn, killed herself with a sword.

Lo clavó en su pecho hermoso
Cayó media agonizante.
Bajo del ombú coposo.) (*AP,* 48)

Her lover's end is just as spectacular:
He jumped up terrified
After the evil had passed
He runs, pulls out the knife
The young lady had expired.
Crazed, blind and confused
He raised the knife high
And plunged it into his chest
With grandiose contempt
Thus was the end of the two
Beneath the bushy *ombú.*

(Levantó atemorizado
Después de pasado el mal
Corre, le arranca el puñal
La joven había espirado.
Loco, ciego y atolondrado
Alto el puñal elevó
En su pecho lo clavó
Con un desprecio grandioso
Así fue el fin de los dos
Bajo del ombú coposo.) (*AP,* 49–50)

In "The Bushy Ombú," the poet incorporates a classic love scene tragedy into the physical environment of the Argentine pampa. This represents a synthesis of the learned and popular traditions in form and content relationships.

In "The Gaucho," Cazón pays homage to a vanishing breed:

Of the gaucho; not even a memory!
Of that type remaining
All go fading away
Like a cursed race
Give it the necessary honor
Because the countryman fought

And gave all of his blood
For this blessed land.

(Del gaucho; ¡ya ni recuerdo!
De ese tipo va quedando
Todos se van acabando
Como una raza maldita
Darle honor se necesita
Porque el paisano luchó
Y toda su sangre dio
Por esta tierra bendita.) (*AP*, 69)

This poem is a virtual roll call of famous gauchos and their participation as active makers of Argentine history. Of course, many gauchos
were of African descent. Throughout the national wars of liberation,
internecine struggles, and pacification of the indigenous peoples, the
gaucho played a significant role. The gaucho's participation in the
formation of the Argentine nation is similar to that of Afro-Argentines
in general:

Look at national events
Search for a deed of war
Where the patriot of this land
Is not represented
Sarmiento—used to say
The last to be rewarded
And the toughest to die.

(Vean los hechos nacionales
Busquen un hecho de guerra,
Que no esté representado
El paisano de esta tierra
Sarmiento—solía decir
El último en recompensas
Y el duro para morir.) (*AP*, 72)

A patriotic, expendable force, the *gaucho* is presented as one who
was willing to give his all for the common good. The same can be said
for the *negro*, whose fate was similar.

Although it is assumed that Cazón was not concerned with the plight of Afro-Argentines, he recognizes their importance in one of his selections. In the preliminary pages to *Joys and Sorrows,* Cazón mentions a collection he has written but apparently never published, entitled "Horas amargas" (Bitter hours), which contains memories dedicated "to the friends of my childhood and to a race that is going away." It is in the poem "Historical Memories: Tucumán and Salta," however, that Cazón pays homage to the brave Afro-Argentines who have sacrificed for the *patria:*

> Also the Ethiopian "Race"
> Which found itself humiliated
> Defended the noble cause
> For freedom they struggled
> They joined together confused
> Differences did not exist;
> For freedom they fought
> For freedom they died.
>
> Those men of color
> Who bit the bullet
> Who did not betray
> Patriots . . . like Falucho
> Many were immortalized
> Believe me! I am proud
> To belong to the race
> Of the freedmen of Cuyo.
>
> (También la Etiópica "Raza"
> Que humillada se encontraron
> Defendió la noble causa
> Por la libertad bregaban
> Confundidas se hermanaban
> Diferencia no existía;
> Por la libertad luchaban
> Por la libertad morían.
>
> Esos hombres de color
> Que mordieron el cartucho

Que no entraron en traición
Patriotas . . . como Falucho
Se inmortalizaron muchos
¡Créanme! que tengo orgullo
Pertenecer a la Raza
De los libertos de Cuyo.) (*AP,* 20–21)

Here, the poet extols the propensity of blacks to be engaged in armed struggle for patriotic reasons. Despite their conditions of bondage, Afro-Argentines fought and died for freedom, a condition elaborated with anaphora, "for freedom." The sacrifices of these historical black heroes are indeed a source of pride and inspiration for the poet in a society that sought to make him and his kind invisible. As a component of the "popular sector," uprooted and displaced, Cazón uses creolism in a nostalgic fashion and as an expression of Afro-Argentine identity. The very title of this volume is indicative of the dualism experienced by Afro-Argentines. As good *criollos* they were able to respond to the demands placed upon them by the country, but as blacks they were never considered integral components of Argentine society.

Luis García Morel

Unlike the work of Higinio Cazón, any reference to the Afro-Argentine experience is absent from the poetry of Luis García Morel. If his intent was to downplay the fact that he was black, this approach did not work, since color was one of the popular topics of his opponents during oral versification contests, as revealed in the episodes cited earlier. Rather than articulate Afro-Argentine concerns in his poetry, García Morel sought an accommodation of black and creole values that reflected national ideology.

The collected poems of Luis García Morel are contained in *Lyric Corners.* This volume is composed of *Alma criolla* (Creole soul), *Poesías populares* (Popular poems), *Cantos de lucha* (Battle songs), *Gauchesco* (The gauchesque), and other poems not previously published in book form. *The Gauchesque* is the only publication by García Morel that exists today as a separate book. Although published in 1937, *Lyric Corners* is characteristic of the *criollista/nativista* tendencies that existed in Argentine literature at the turn of this century.

Victor di Santo, in his study of the *payador,* extols the accomplishments of this talented performer: "Luis García who in his expanded trajectory presented himself indifferently as García Morel or Morel García as we have seen, is considered unanimously on both banks of the River Plate, the best *payador* of all time."[9] In the list of *payadas* included in the appendix of Di Santo's book, which covers the years 1884–1925, he does not list a confrontation between Ezeiza and García Morel, which would have given one or the other bragging rights to the River Plate (Plata) region. They both defeated Ramón Viejtes at different moments in their careers. Whether García Morel was the best *payador* of all time is debatable, given the career of Ezeiza and his documented exploits.

García Morel's poetry is thematically diverse within the *criollo* tradition as he concentrates upon memory, love, and Argentine culture. Poems such as "La guitarra" (The guitar), "El payador" (The payador), and "De mi tierra" (From my land) exemplify the author's penchant for popular motifs. "The Guitar" is a poem of cultural synthesis:

> The guitar controls itself
> it is the lyre of the race
> which joins two worlds
> delicate and captivating;
> a moorish conquerer
> of Spanish sentiments
> it arrives in pampa arms
> of America, light of love,
> and backs up the payador
> during country songs.
>
> Guitar of the awakening
> of the songs of the River Plate
> adorned the serenade
> in the garden of the home;
> clear and small altar
> to lift up hearts

9. Victor Di Santo, *El canto del payador en el circo criollo,* 121. Di Santo writes that the real name of this individual was Luis Dionisio García Morel.

to the worthy emotions
of the true loved ones
has its trills moderated
with heavenly illusions.

It has a bit of jungle and of dawn
so much hidden harmony
that incites the virtuoso
with surprises it possesses;
flowering murmurer
a small enchanted orchestra
on winged inspiration
of grandeur, which follow
the domains of God
on a mighty journey.

The guitar, loyal tribute
of sublime beauty
which sweetens sadness
with lyricism for fruit;
How many times in a minute
it evokes its lovable accent!
As in ecstasy
for who interprets and loves it,
it relives the great panorama
of song, of feeling.

(La guitarra se enseñorea,
es la lira de la raza
que dos mundos entrelaza
mimosa y cautivadora;
morisca conquistadora
de sentimientos hispanos,
llega a los brazos pampeanos
de América, luz de amor,
y secunda al payador
en poemas campechanos.

Guitarra del despertar
de las canciones del Plata,

adornó la serenata
en el jardín del hogar;
sonoro y pequeño altar
para elevar corazones
a las dignas emociones
de los bien enamorados,
tiene sus trinos templados
con celestes ilusiones.

Tiene de selva y de aurora
tanta armonía escondida,
que al virtuoso lo convida
con sorpresas que atesora;
floreciente arrulladora,
pequeña orquesta encantada
en la inspiración alada
de celsitud, que va en pos
de los dominios de Dios
en prodigiosa jornada.

La guitarra, fiel tributo
de las sublimes bellezas
que dulcifican tristezas
con el lirismo por fruto;
¡cuánto tiempo en un minuto
evoca su amable acento!
Cómo en un arrobamiento
de quien la interpreta y la ama,
revive el gran panorama
del cantar, del sentimiento.)[10]

The guitar is an element of harmony in a society where two opposing peoples, conquered and conquerers, exist in an environment of tension and cultural imposition. A product of the biological fusion in this equation is the gaucho *payador* whose songs keep alive the oral tradition. Once the historic relevance of the guitar is established in the first stanza,

10. Luis García, *Esquinas líricas: versos*, 42–43. Subsequent references will appear in the text as *EL*.

the poet's attention turns to the romantic mode replete with images of serenades and lovers. A transition from the local to the universal occurs in the third stanza through the analogy "small enchanted orchestra" in search of "the dominions of God," which elevates this instrument to a higher plane and then leaves it as a lyrical vehicle of feeling.

Like Cazón, García Morel dedicates a poem to the profession of *payador.* His focus, however, is the traditional rural singer rather than the urban professional:

> The *payador* is a bard
> of the rural environment
> where the Argentinc people raised
> its shout of liberty;
> the time of the colony
> saw him rise up on his farm
> perhaps forging for the Inca
> a new majesty.
>
> He sang about the tenderness of love
> poetic sleepless nights
> sighs and laughs
> of emotional intention;
> then the history of the gaucho
> filled with heroic deeds
> with pieces of sentiments
> larger than reason.
>
> If Vega were not a Homer,
> it's because another aspect of history
> changed from mission and glory
> to national rhapsody;
> and an Aristarco was not lacking
> who would unite polishing
> the verses that kept on guarding
> our oral tradition.
>
> The Martín Fierro, of Hernández
> country philosophies
> colored the old trenches
> with cannon fodder;

and the Lázaro, of Gutiérrez
tells us with pride
that the bard of our nation
is not an insolent gaucho.

(El payador, es un bardo
del ambiente campesino
donde alzó el pueblo argentino
su grito de libertad;
el tiempo del colonaje
lo vio surgir en su finca,
quizá forjándole al Inca
una nueva majestad.

Cantó al amor sus ternuras
poéticas trasnochadas
suspiros y carcajadas
de emocionante intención;
luego, la historia del gaucho
llena de heróicos alientos
con trozos de sentimientos
más grandes que la razón.

Si Vega, no fue un Homero,
es que otra faz de la historia
cambió de misión y gloria
al rapsoda nacional;
y no faltó un Aristarco,
que uniera pulimentando
los versos que iba guardando
nuestra tradición oral.

El Martín Fierro, de Hernández,
filosofías camperas,
pinta las viejas trincheras
con la carne de cañón;
y el Lázaro, de Gutiérrez,
nos relata dignamente,
que no es un gaucho insolente
el bardo de mi nación.)

The poem's first four stanzas extol the virtues of the gaucho from colonialism to the nineteenth century, presenting this figure as a major force in the battle for liberation. The poet correctly relates the gaucho phenomenon of oral poetry to the broader classical context of the Western tradition while demonstrating a keen awareness of national history:

> Along comes cosmopolitanism
> it brings us its traditions,
> its flutes, its accordions
> and its *troveros* in pairs,
> that's because in all the towns,
> sons of an environment,
> there is a song one feels
> like the voice of the paternal home.
>
> The happy Spaniards,
> who are noted patriots,
> their *malagüeñas* and *jotas*
> lend heartfelt pride,
> the Cubans their *guajiras,*
> the Filipinos their *tangos,*
> And Uruguayans and Argentines
> this old tradition.
>
> It is the country of the good song,
> everything is Italian greatness:
> German is Wagnerian
> although before it was judged bad;
> and France, the enchantress,
> which is more and more French,
> it is felt in Marseille
> that even Russia was triumphant.
>
> (Viene el cosmopolitismo
> nos trae con sus tradiciones,
> sus gaitas sus acordeones
> y sus troveros al par,
> es porque en todos los pueblos,
> hijos de su medio ambiente,

hay un canto que se siente
cual la voz del patrio hogar.

Los alegres españoles,
que son insignes patriotas,
sus malagüeñas y jotas
estiman de corazón,
los cubanos us guajiras,
sus tangos los filipinos,
y Uruguayos y Argentinos
esta vieja tradición.

Es la patria del bel canto,
toda es grandeza italiana:
Alemania, es Wagneriana
aunque antes lo juzgó mal;
y Francia, la encantadora,
que es cada vez más francesa,
se siente en la Marsellesa
que hasta Rusia fue triunfal.)

Here there is a subtle criticism by the poet of what he views as cultural intrusion. In spite of immigration, urbanization, and international influence, the gaucho has prevailed. This is due primarily to his popular focus:

Payador, singer of the people,
who has a little bit of science.
The poetry of the countryside
with half a world at your feet
the concert of the jungle
the voice of the Argentine gaucho,
and a ray of divine sun
of eighteen ten.

It is not'a payador he who wishes
nor he who sings nonsense,
as much as he imitates the trills
of the whining simpleton;
the name without deeds is not enough,

nor begged fame,
instead a mind inspired
by natural intuition.

(Payador, cantor del pueblo,
que tiene de ciencia un lampo.
La poesía del campo
con medio mundo a sus pies
el concierto de la selva
la voz del gaucho argentino,
y un rayo del sol divino
de mil ochocientos diez.

No es payador el que quiere
ni el que canta desatinos,
por más que imite los trinos
del quejumbroso zorzal;
ni basta el nombre sin hechos,
ni la fama mendigada,
sino la mente inspirada
por intuición natural.) (*EL*, 103-6)

"High," imported culture does not detract from the national appeal of the indigenous singer. In "The Payador," García Morel elaborates upon the history of this Argentine popular figure, relating him to the fight for independence, the solidification of the gaucho myth, his worldly counterparts, and his role in the nation's culture. The image of this figure remains deeply embedded in the nation's psyche.

"From My Land" is a poignant tribute to the earth. Anaphora with "I bring" conveys the sense of the protagonist as an embodiment of values inherent within the context. What he brings is intangible, but represents the essence of the life interpreted in the poem, which is that of rural culture:

I bring from the late evenings
the shadows, that fall dying,
the rumor of the fountains
and the Ay! of the little birds;
I bring from the love songs

amorous illusions
of the flashy gauchos
who show in the stirrups,
the tradition of my land
which brightens the heart.

I bring faraway memories
that have ceased for some,
glories that others conquered
and which today serve as advice;
I bring sparks and reflections
of the furrows of the road,
where destiny hides
in each grain of sand,
like a history of suffering
of the noble Argentine gaucho.

(Traigo de las tardecitas
las sombras, que caen murientes,
el rumor de las vertientes
y el ¡ay! de las avecitas;
traigo de las vidalitas
amorosas ilusiones,
de los gauchos guapetones
que se lucen en la hierra,
la tradición de mi tierra
que alegra a los corazones.

Traigo recuerdos añejos
que para algunos cesaron,
glorias que otros conquistaron
y que hoy sirven de consejos;
traigo chispas y reflejos
de las huellas del camino,
de dónde oculta el destino
en cada grano de arena,
como una historia de pena
del noble gaucho argentino.)

    The poetic voice serves as a type of collective memory of the gaucho spirit, accentuating the intangible aspects of this myth. There is strong identification with the creole spirit and an articulation of positive rural values.

> I bring fresh harmony
> of the sly fellow and the ox driver,
> because I fear that the country dweller
> might carry them to faraway places;
> I bring old fantasies,
> savage memories,
> and imposing homages
> for the brave ones, who in excess
> have given for progress
> flowering countrysides.
>
> I bring the investments
> of the payador of the pampas,
> of the sun which kisses his face
> fibers of love and sweetness;
> I bring a song of adventures
> of the traveling cart,
> which in the rural solitude
> loses its last vision
> more creole than a *pericón* dance
> poorer than a shack.
>
> (Traigo frescas armonías
> del zorzal y del boyero,
> porque temo que el pampero
> las lleve a otras lejanías;
> traigo viejas fantasías,
> recordaciones salvajes,
> e imponencias de homenajes
> a los bravos, que en exceso
> han dado para el progreso
> floraciones de paisajes.
>
> Traigo las investiduras
> del payador de la pampa,
> del sol que besa su estampa
> fibras de amor y dulzuras;
> traigo un canto de aventuras

> de la carreta viajera,
> que en la soledad campera
> pierde su última visión,
> más criolla que un pericón,
> más pobre que una tapera.) (*EL,* 78–79)

The poet's vision is summed up in the last two verses: "More creole than a *pericón* / poorer than a shack." This attitude represents the overall *criollista* worldview implicit in the poetry of García Morel, who constantly sought the essence of "lo argentino." It was to be a country of diverse groups where a nonproblematic existence was possible because of the unifying factor of *criollismo,* minus questions regarding ethnicity and color. Unfortunately, Afro-Argentines were the last to understand the pervasive nature of this social ideology.

Gabino Ezeiza

In an article entitled "Gabino Ezeiza: verdad y leyenda" (Gabino Ezeiza: truth and legend), Luis Soler Cañas presents a coherent discussion of the life and times of Gabino Ezeiza. Soler Cañas mentions numerous sources for his facts, but never provides concrete documentation for important events in Ezeiza's life, such as his affiliation with *La Juventud.* Soler Cañas states: "Those dates allow me to affirm that at the beginning of the year 1876 Gabino Ezeiza appears as a poet in a Buenos Aires newspaper which counts him, besides, among its promoters and editors. In addition, he is in charge as chronicler or reporter, of the news section. In the unfindable pages today of that newspaper, Gabino is as author or as personality of the chronicle, a constant presence."[11] Soler Cañas is referring to Ezeiza's affiliation with *La Juventud* between 1876 and 1878, a period during which he

11. Luis Soler Cañas, "Gabino Ezeiza: verdad y leyenda," 67. Nestor Ortiz Oderigo, an Argentine who has done serious research on the black population in that country, writes regarding Gabino Ezeiza: "He was an educated man. His pen produced theatrical pieces like *Lucía Miranda* and the novelistic work *The Branch of Flowers.* He exercised, besides, journalism. It is calculated at more than five hundred the number of pages left by the artist, in addition to many dispersed, that some day will have to be collected." *Aspectos de la cultura africana en el Río de la Plata,* 116.

was a constant contributor, publishing a fine selection of lyric poetry. Soler Cañas's discussion of Ezeiza and his works is representative of the critical attitude taken toward him to the degree that only his work as *payador* is mentioned. This is evident in such books as *El cantar del payador* (The song of the payador), *Diccionario de payadores* (Dictionary of payadores), *Itinerario del payador* (Itinerary of the payador), *El arte de los payadores* (The art of the payador) and *El canto del payador en el circo criollo* (The song of the payador in the creole circus), which are listed in the bibliography of this study. Ezeiza's artistry, however, transcends the popular performance phase and earns him the right to be discussed as "poet" as well.

Ezeiza was not just a *payador* poet in the *repentista,* or spontaneous oral tradition. He was also a constant contributor to the intellectual well-being of the black community. His popular poems "Saludo a Paysandú" (Greetings to Paysandú), "El paisano" (The countryman), and "El rastri-ador" (The tracker) are included in most recent anthologies of gaucho poetry. Argentine literary historians, however, have not been as kind, since the few references to Ezeiza as poet that I have been able to find are not positive. Typical is Roberto Giusti, who does not mention Ezeiza and those of his ilk in an adulation of the Argentine gaucho myth: "While the true gaucho diminished . . . , the literary gaucho tradition was born in the suburbs of the city, whose long descent of a bastard native immediatcly hybrid with the *cocolichesca* and other suburban species, populated multiple little notebooks with a cheap literature, which had popular rhymers, the most disseminated among them the black *payador* Gabino Ezeiza."[12] The problem here lies in the classic erroneous distinction between "popular" and "learned" poets, a difference based, in this case, upon social class and ethnicity. Ezeiza was a poet, a cultivator of verse in both traditions. This versatility is evident in several poems included in *La Juventud* in 1876: "A orillas del Plata" (On the banks of the River Plate), "El viento de amor" (The wind of love), "Las artes" (The arts), "Amor filial" (Filial love), "Al poeta el desgraciado" (To the wretched poet), and "A Montevideo" (To Montevideo). These selections demonstrate flexibility in form and content as well as the

12. Included in Rafael Alberto Arrieta, ed., *Historia de la literatura argentina,* 529.

author's ability to synthesize European and creole worldviews. Since
Ezeiza is normally associated with *gaucho* poetry, "On the Banks of
the River Plate" will demonstrate a previously unknown side of his
verse:

A sailor rowed
from the River Plate to the shore
in a little boat
with incredible zeal
cutting the waves
which upon seeing themselves conquered
go and roughened
crash upon the shore.

But the boat arrives
from the waters on the side
happily he has arrived
and jumped to the shore,
The sailor is happy
his face all smiles
and then within an instant
the boat he tied.

With a sure step
almost at a trot
he crossed the shoreline
then he stopped.

At a little house
of poor appearance
then with his hands
he clapped his palms.

A window opened
and there appeared
a beautiful young lady.

Who goes there? she asked
(the sailor answered)
It is I precious jewel;
the door opened.

(Bogaba un marino
del Plata a la orilla
en una barquilla
con increíble afán
cortando las alas
que al verse vencidas
van y embravecidas
en las toscas dan.

Mas llega la barca,
de la tosca al lado,
feliz ha llegado,
y a tierra saltó,

Alegre el marino
risueño el semblante
y luego al instante
la barca amarró.

Con paso seguro
casi a la carrera
cruzó la ribera
luego se paró.

En una casita
de pobre apariencia
luego con las manos
las palmas batió.

Se abrió una ventana
y apareció a ella
una joven bella.

¿Quién va? preguntó:
[contestó el marino]
yo soy prenda amada;
la puerta se abrió.)[13]

13. Gabino Ezeiza, "A Orillas del Plata," *La Juventud* 1, 1 (enero 1876): 2. Gabino
Ezeiza published in *La Juventud* the following poems: "A Orillas del Plata," 1, 1 (1876):

"On the Banks of the River Plate," a love poem, is written in *Arte menor* (two to eight syllables) in the classic style of the *octavilla*, a version of the Italian octave. This poem is a clear indication of Ezeiza's familiarity with the "learned" poetic tradition, as well as his ability to adapt traditional form to local content by creating an archetypal love scene on the La Plata estuary.

In this initial phase of his work, Ezeiza devotes poems to such diverse topics as love, immortality, the creative process, time, and friendship. The tone, thematics, and style are of the romantic mode, with emphasis upon emotional status. The uplifting capacity of creative endeavors is the theme of "The Arts":

> Letters which demonstrate
> A thousand immortal goods,
> Conquered they are riches
> of laws and labor:
> with them reason is armed
> with invincible shields,
> unfading goods
> of freedom and love.
>
> With them, teaching
> expands and flourishes
> and wisdom explains to us
> the fruits of peace;
> the mother she is of the arts,
> which in a superb link
> presents to the human being
> virtue without disguise.
>
> (Las letras que demuestran
> Mil bienes inmortales,
> Conquistas son reales
> de leyes y labor:
> con ellas razón se arma

2; "Amor Filial," 8 (1876): 2; "Al poeta el desgraciado," 1, 12 (1876): 2; "A Montevideo," 1, 25 (1876): 1–2. During the second epoch of *La Juventud,* Ezeiza published "La tortola" and "Cuál viento ya pasó" in 1 (1877): 2; "Oh que vive Dios" and "¿Para que lloran?" in 3 (1877): 2; "¡Qué bella diedad!" in 7 (1878): 4, and "La unión" in 12 (1878): 3.

de escudos invencibles,
bienes inmarcesibles
de libertad y amor.

Con ellas, la enseñanza
se estiende y fructifica,
y sabia nos esplica
los frutos de la paz;
la madre es ella de artes,
que en lazo soberano,
presentan al humano
virtudes sin disfraz.)[14]

The poet views artists and their work as noble because it gives humans the capacity to create and to rise above worldly concerns without being immune to them. Subsequently, immortality and invincibility are essential to liberty and love. At the same time, the teaching and wisdom implicit in the arts can make a better world.

The maximum expression of Ezeiza's romanticism is found in "Meditación" (Meditation). This selection, a contemplation of life and death, the fleetingness of existence, is a verbalization of many romantic notions.

Which is the difficult moment
That with mad dementia
The weight of existence
We wish to abandon?
When hope is lost
For that illusion one seeks
The imagination is dazzled
Beginning to meditate . . . ?

We meditate that life
Is a temporary illusion
Meditating that chimera
We lose our calmness
And the dazzled reason
Which cowardliness incites

14. Gabino Ezeiza, "Las artes," *La Juventud* 1, no. 6 (6 de febrero 1876): 2.

You believe that only there exists
Calmness in the tomb.

Fatal suicide then
Is presented before our eyes
And in the grave your remains
We believe find calm and peace
It is an abyss we probe
Only because perhaps
When we take those steps
It may open beneath our feet.

(¿Cuál es el penoso instante
que con furiosa demencia
El peso de la existencia
Queremos abandonar?
Que perdida la esperanza
De aquella ilusión que busca
La imaginación se ofusca
Empezando a meditar . . . ?

Meditamos que la vida
Es ilusión pasajera
Meditando esa quimera
Perdemos nuestra quietud
Y la razón ofuscada
Qué cobardía rebiste
Creos tan solo que existe
La calma en el ataúd:

Al suicidio fatal luego
Se presenta a nuestros ojos
Y en la tumba sus despojos
Cremos hallar calma y paz
Y es abismo que sondeamos
Tan solamente al travez
Que cuando esos pasos damos
Se habre bajo nuestros pies.)[15]

15. Gabino Ezeiza, "Meditación," *La Juventud* 2d época, no. 2 (20 de diciembre 1877): 3.

Dementia and death to alleviate pressures inherent in the human condition establish the tone in the first verses, which flow into the retrospective "meditation" of the title. Meditation and contemplation are preoccupations of the romantic poet as well as the suicide motif. Images of instability—"fleeting illusion," "chimera"—foreshadow the sense of loss of "calm" and "reason" in the second stanza, culminating in the sense that peace is achievable only in death—"tomb."

The accumulation of funeral imagery terminates in "suicide" as the only option to an intolerable existence ("And in the grave his remains / we believe will find peace and quiet"). The disillusionment in this poem by Ezeiza is characteristic of the romantic mode in literature. Whether an argument can be made for the poet's dissatisfaction with his society is arguable since it is apparent that Ezeiza is following romantic conventions, but at the same time he is the product of an indifferent set of social circumstances that he tries to correct.

The transition of Ezeiza from romantic poet to *payador* is addressed by Soler Cañas in *Orígenes de la literatura lunfarda* (Origins of underground literature). While making the distinction between the "classic" and "urban" *payadores,* Soler Cañas writes, "the urban *payador,* in general, is professionalized. If the classic *payador* sang and in payment for his art was given hospitality, a bed and food—that at least we must suppose—the urban *payador* is a professional artist who performs his art in exchange for a monetary stipend . . . He has in general a preestablished itinerary in which towns and cities alternate when not his own with that of the circus manager who has contracted him."[16] These attitudes mirror both the aforementioned attitudes of *La Broma* regarding the professionalization of Ezeiza's craft and the apparent disgust of Roberti Giusti regarding the demise of the traditional *payador.* Soler Cañas informs us that within the urban context, Ezeiza made excellent use of the print media in communicating with his audience.

Ezeiza was, indeed, a very prolific poet who produced an extraordinary amount of poetry, some of which has survived in the forms of book, chapbooks, and periodicals. The most complete listing of Ezeiza's works is found in Adolfo Prieto's *Creole Discourse in the Formation of*

16. Luis Soler Cañas, *Orígenes de la literatura lunfarda,* 150–51.

Modern Argentina, which contains an "Indice de la Biblioteca Criollo de Roberto Lehman-Nitsche" that lists sixteen works either by or about Ezeiza.[17]

For the purposes of this study, I will refer to seven volumes of poetry by Gabino Ezeiza that vary in length and complexity: *Canciones del payador Gabino Ezeiza* (Songs of the payador Gabino Ezeiza, 2d series, 1885); *Cantares criollas por Gabino Ezeiza, payador argentino* (Creole songs by Gabino Ezeiza, Argentine payador, 1886); *Canciones del payador argentino Gabino Ezeiza: nueva y última colección* (Songs of the Argentine payador Gabino Ezeiza: new and latest collection, 2d part, 1892); *Mi guitarra* (My guitar, 1895); *Canciones del payador Gabino Ezeiza* (Songs of the payador Gabino Ezeiza, 1896); *Nuevas canciones inéditas del payador argentino Gabino Ezeiza* (New unpublished songs of the Argentine payador Gabino Ezeiza, 1897); and *Colección de canciones del payador argentino Gabino Ezeiza* (Collection of songs by the Argentine payador Gabino Ezeiza, 1897). Collectively, these works are representative of the *criollista* dimension of Ezeiza's poetry. Some of the poems are repeated from volume to volume.

Songs of the Payador Gabino Ezeiza contains a dozen poems whose titles reflect their content. They are "La guitarra" (The guitar), "La muerte de Moyano" (The death of Moyano), "Fantasía" (Fantasy), "Don Juan," "El volcán" (The volcano), "La pailita" (The little pan), "Recuerdos" (Memories), "Los ayes de un veterano" (The sighs of a veteran), "Las noches del alma" (Nights of the soul), "Vega y Dolores" (Vega and Dolores), "A mi amigo Trejo" (To my friend Trejo), and "Dos extremos" (Two extremes). As a popular poet, Ezeiza demonstrates constantly his ability to versify a number of topics that appeal to a wide audience. In the introductory remarks to this volume addressed "A mi amigo Sansón Carrasco" (To my friend Sansón Carrasco), Ezeiza clarifies his position in regard to his craft: "The greatest desire of my life will always be song. Poetry, a power which only nature deposits in certain beings, like the essence in flowers, and which nevertheless, like a diamond, one must polish so that there may be presented in all of its phases that which

17. Prieto, *El discurso criollista,* 214–16.

before hid its brilliance."[18] Ezeiza singles out his innate ability and his desire as the primary factors that have led to his success. His life has been devoted to honing his craft. Ezeiza continues, "Yet, if the craftsman lacks the material to do it, I lack the necessary study, even when nature gave me the capacity to be able to improvise one or another quartet, and not having been able to obtain due to a thousand circumstances the necessary polish, I submit to your wise ideas these poor verses, not as a work of art, but as an uncultured bard who sings because he sings, like a bird does in a thicket." Ever humble regarding himself and his origins, Gabino Ezeiza makes the point that poetry is not the exclusive domain of the educated and that the success of the popular poet is due more to practical experience than to formal training.

As the titles suggest, these poems vary from surface concerns to the more introspective musings of the poet. "The Volcano" equates the eruptive power of this natural process to pent-up human emotions:

> Volcano that my heart encloses
> Whose eruption I feel
> Black abyss of torment
> Which I brought to the world:
> Erupts here with violence
> And the pain I feel
> Forms another crude torment
> Like nobody imagined.
>
> (Volcán que mi pecho encierra
> Cuya erupción yo presiento,
> Negro abismo del tormento
> Que al mundo lo traje yo;
> Estalla aquí con violencia
> Y del dolor que yo siento
> Forma otro crudo tormento
> Como nadie imaginó.) (*CP*, 26)

"Memories" addresses the issue of the poet's competence in an indifferent and uncaring environment:

---

18. Gabino Ezeiza, *Canciones del payador Gabino Ezeiza,* 2d serie, 5. Subsequent references will appear in the text as *CP.*

Some are born with the star
Of living dead with laughter,
With that single goal
Fun and pleasure
They feel neither pain nor pleasure,
Nothing matters to them,
Saying: life is short
The same today as yesterday.

I understand that everything
I lack to be a poet
Like the painter his palette
And a sculptor his tool.

If I don't have polish
Never will I make good verses,
I will be an owl without a watchman
Or a lamp without oil.

(Unos nacen con la estrella
De vivir muertos de risa,
Con esta sola divisa:
La diversión y el placer

No sienten pena ni agrado,
A ellos nada les importa,
Diciendo: la vida es corta,
Lo mismo es hoy que ayer.

Yo comprendo de que todo
Me falta para ser poeta,
Como a un pintor la paleta
Y a un escultor el buril.

Si no tengo pulimento
Nunca he de hacer versos buenos,
Seré chuza sin sereno
O sin aceite un candil.) (CP, 33)

There is mild criticism of inequality by the poet in this instance. At
the same time, he is aware of his real or imagined inadequacies. This

poem conveys basically the same message as the introductory remarks in this volume, which were commented upon earlier in this study.

"Nights of the Soul" confronts the issue of death:

> One night I enjoyed
> As many others, the night air
> Barely a little cloud
> Appeared in the west
>   Which slowly growing
> The sky became cloudy
> I listened to harsh thunder
> And then, it darkened.
>
> The space for moments
> The lightning illuminates
> Wherever the ray strikes . . .
> The water begins to fall.
>   My poor mother, who then
> Enjoyed sweet life
> Was wounded by the sickle
> Passed from being to not being.
>
> (Gozaba yo en una noche
> Como otras tantas, serena:
> Una nubecilla apenas
> En Occidente asomó,
>   Que lentamente creciendo
> El cielo lo fue empañando,
> Fui ronco trueno escuchando
> Y después, oscureció.
>
> El espacio por momentos
> El relámpago ilumina;
> Doquier el rayo fulmina . . .
> El agua empieza a caer.
>   Mi pobre madre, que entonces.
> Gozaba de dulce vida,
> Fue por la segur herida
> Pasó del ser al no ser.) (*CP,* 43)

This poem recounts a personal tragedy of Ezeiza, and like several others in the collection, is emotionally charged and sensitive. The imagery is nocturnal, celestial, part of a metaphoric environment whose outcome is tragic.

Creole Songs by Gabino Ezeiza, Argentine Payador contains thirteen selections: "El sabia" (The sabia), "La caridad" (Charity), "El esclavo" (The slave), "Horas tristes" (Sad hours), "Gratitud" (Gratitude), "La carne con cuero" (Meat with hide), "El viejito Montoya" (Old Montoya), "Canciones varias" (Several songs), "Ausencia y duda" (Absence and doubt), "Un percance" (A misfortune), "Mi caudal" (My wealth), "Adiós a Melo" (Goodbye to Melo), and "Reunión amena" (Joyful reunion). These representative selections explore human emotions, solitude, companionship, and interactions. "The Sabia" is a poem of wandering, solitude, and contemplation in which the sabia bird exacerbates the sense of loneliness experienced by the poet. The poet is aware of other birds who accompany him in his solitude, but this particular one holds special meaning:

> It does not have like other birds
> The splendid clothing
> Of a blended plumage
> Like the sunflower
> It does not have a golden beak
> But in hours of rest
> It seems more beautiful to us
> Although dark in its color.
>
> When I have sung out my grief
> With pain and emotional
> More than a sigh has been directed
> By the one who thought she understood me
> While singing out my bitterness
> I was singing those of others
> And I have seen from time to time
> A tear flow.
>
> (No tiene como otras aves
> El espléndido ropaje
> De un matizado plumaje

Como tiene el mirasol.
No tiene un dorado pico,
Mas en horas de reposo
Nos parece más hermoso,
Aunque pardo en su color.

Cuando he cantado mi pena
Con dolor y emocionado
Más de un suspiro ha lanzado
Quien me supo comprender;
Al cantar mis amarguras
Las de otros iba cantando
Y he visto de cuando en cuando
Una lágrima correr.) (*CP,* 5)

In this instance, human emotions are projected upon the natural environment in an attempt to alleviate some of the pressures inherent in being rootless—the situation of the protagonist of this poem. There is an implied analogy between the image of a bird who is perceived as an outcast and the black poetic persona.

The issues of human suffering and compassion are addressed in the poem "The Slave." Narrated from the perspective of the bondsman, the selection emphasizes collective freedom. The sense of loss is both physical and spiritual, effectively obliterating self-esteem and, more tragically, destroying families:

Of the children I had
The two of them were born slaves
And my owners sold them
Where will I find them?
How will I be able to protect them
If barely adolescents
They are dragging around chains
As I wear them on my feet.

(De los hijos que tenía
Los dos esclavos nacieron
Y mis amos los vendieron
¿Dónde los encontraré?

En qué podré protejerlos
Si adolescentes apenas
Van arrastrando cadenas
Como yo las llevo al pie.) (*CC*, 15)

The impotence and frustration incurred during two generations of slavery is addressed in this poem. The narrative perspective of this poem is the first person and rightly so, since this way the poet is able to convey a more intense feeling of imprisonment and dehumanization. Death is preferable to bondage in an environment of total negation of personhood:

There is nothing for me! eternal night
Of misfortune! a star
I find neither the beautiful moon
Nor the Sun's brilliance;
I don't find essence in the flowers.
Nor feel the palm trees moan
There's only this shout in my soul:
You are the slave of a master.

(No hay para mí! noche eterna
De desventura! una estrella,
Ni encuentro la luna bella
Ni tiene lampos el Sol;
No hallo esencia en las flores,
Ni siento jemir la palma
Solo hay este grito en mi alma:
Esclavo eres de un señor.)

In direct discourse, the poet denounces the institution of slavery and its negative impact upon the human condition. Anaphora with "no" and "neither" exacerbates the loss of self-esteem and individualism perpetrated by this system.

A considerable amount of this volume is devoted to the errant life of the gaucho. Many commonplaces of this mode of existence are evident in the poem "Meat with Hide":

Between a column of smoke
Which rises in a spiral

Under the elegant foliage
Of the most corpulent ombú
Is the owner of the ranch
Giving the necessary order
Because he sees the people arriving
With enough certainty.

There are three previous gauchos
Who have come earlier
And they are found man to man
Breaking the wild pony.
While one drinks mate
The other tells a story
And the other one stirs the fire
With his knife.

There is an awning hung between
The ombú and a stick
Which is not all bad
Because the sun beams down.
The meat cooks are there
Like bakers
Making fierce grimaces
Because they are burning from the heat.

(Entre una columna de humo
Que en espiral se levanta,
Bajo la gallarda planta
Del más corpulento ombú,
Está el dueno de la estancia
Dando la orden conveniente
Porque acudir ve la gente
Con bastante exactitud.

Hay tres gauchos prevenidos
Que han venido más temprano
Y se encuentran mano a mano
Prendiéndole al cimarrón.
Mientras que uno toma mate
El otro cuenta algún cuento
Y el otro el fuego al momento
Atiza con el facón.

> Hay un toldo sostenido
> En el ombú y en un palo,
> El cual no es del todo malo
> Porque atajan algo al sol.
> Allí están los asadores
> De la carne como horneros
> Haciendo visajes fieros
> Porque se asan de calor.) (*CC*, 22)

The symbolic solitary *ombú* tree, the *estancia*, the half-wild *cimarrón* pony, the impending beef *asado,* all symbols of gaucho life, set the stage for the forthcoming tests of skills. The gaucho remains an essential motif within the *criollista* mode of the era that the author interprets. Ezeiza and García Morel are consistent in their interpretations of this Argentine myth.

In *Creole Songs,* Ezeiza explores a plethora of themes common to Argentine culture. A sense of alienation is combined with an examination of social topics expressed in popular verse form that is characteristic of the oral dimension of Ezeiza's works.

Songs of the Argentine Payador Gabino Ezeiza: New and Latest Collection consists of a dozen selections that reflect thematic variety similar to his other texts. The titles include "A mi guitarra" (To my guitar), "A Gervasio Méndez" (To Gervasio Méndez), "Locura" (Craziness), "El Calvario" (Calvary), "El General José María Paz" (General José María Paz), "Razonemos" (Let's reason), "Enfermo" (Sick), "Firulete" (Firulete), "Ahí estás" (There you are), "Batalla de Maipo" (Battle of Maipu), "¿Te acuerdas tú?" (Do you remember?) and "Canción" (Song). Religion, patriotism, love, and everyday occurrences are within the purview of this volume.

"To My Guitar" conjures up images of the poet's connection to the African oral tradition:

> If from some faraway thunder
> I felt the vague rumor
> Your strings repeated it
> Without overlooking the place
> And when during nights of insomnia

I did not reconcile with sleep
I took you eagerly
In order to begin to sing.

   (Si de algún trueno lejano
El vago rumor sentía,
Tus cuerdas lo repetían
No dando a duda lugar;
Y cuando en noches de insomnio
Yo no conciliaba con el sueño
Te tomaba con empeño
Para ponerme a cantar.)[19]

The faraway thunder that inspires the vague rumbling appears to be symbolic references to ancestry, although the poem's literal meaning is clear. While the drum is often presented as an instrument that connects Africa to the Americas, in Argentina it is replaced, in some instances, by the guitar.

Another poem that deals with poetry and its inspiration is "There You Are":

   There you are unsettled lyre . . .
Since I have abandoned you
I have awakened from lethargy
To return to play you:
Why to the slightest sound
Your accent vibrates so softly
When I took the oath
Not to play you again?

   (Ahí estás lira colgada . . .
Desde que te he abandonado
Del letargo he despertado
Para volverte a pulsar:
¿Por qué al más pequeño ruido
Vibra muy tenue tu acento,

---

19. Gabino Ezeiza, *Canciones del payador argentino Gabino Ezeiza: nueva y última colección,* 3. Subsequent references will appear in the text as *NC.*

Cuando yo hice el juramento
De no volverte a pulsar?) (*NC,* 25)

The poet's creative impulse is personified and presented as having abandoned its creator. The poet's attitude is one of regret as he remembers past positive experiences that have resulted in temporary rewards. A series of important questions are raised in the exchange between poet and lyre:

Why if I have an idea
Which agitates in my brain
And at each step shouts to me
Must you silence the lyre?
Why, if so much in life
I have worked for morally
Have I not longed for
Material work?

(¿Por qué si tengo una idea
Que en mi cerebro se agita
Y a cada paso me grita:
"Debes la lira colgar?"
¿Por qué, si tanto en la vida
Moralmente he trabajado,
No debo de haber ansiado
El trabajo material?)

The conflict here is between the ideal and the material, that is, the choice between creative activity and earning a living. In this instance, there is not a happy medium between the two activities. In real life, however, the poet did resolve that dilemma.

My Guitar: Happy Verses, Stories, Tales, etc. (1895) consists of "Old Montoya," "Meat with Hide," "My Wealth," "Joyful Reunion," "Several Songs," "Absence and Doubt," and "Goodbye to Melo." The first two selections extol the virtues of gaucho life. "My Wealth" is a penetrating look at a destitute individual:

Two cents and a cigarette
Constitute my riches,

A candleholder, a table,
A chair and a pillow.
From my mind burst forth
The most cruel disappointments,
Thus in these papers
I make an improvisation.

(Dos centavos y un cigarro
Constituye mi riqueza,
Un candelero, una mesa,
Una silla y un colchón.
Después de mi mente brotan
Los desengaños más crueles,
Así es que en estos papeles
Hago una improvisación.)[20]

Destitute and disillusioned, the poet reflects upon a life of hard times
that has had more than just a physical impact:

Another pile of papers
That I call my poetry
Where there is suffering and happiness
All mixed up at the same time.
Letters, episodes, poems,
Brilliant declarations
Are found in this instant
Scattered with my passions.

(Otro montón de papeles
Que yo llamo mis poesías
Donde hay penas y alegrías
Todo revuelto a la vez.
Cartas, episodios, poemas,
Declaraciones brillantes,
Se encuentran en este instante
Esparcidos a mis pasiones.) (*MG*, 18)

20. Gabino Ezeiza, *Mi guitarra: versos alegres, cuentos, historias, etc.*, 16. Subsequent
references will appear in the text as *MG*.

The true wealth of the poet resides not in his material possessions but rather in the treasures of his creative output. His production is diverse, which corresponds with the trials and tribulations of a complex lifestyle. Ezeiza, who lived well much of his life, died in poverty in 1916. Perhaps "My Wealth" reflects an earlier stage while at the same time foretelling his destiny.

"Various Songs" and "Absence and Doubt" are poems of love and longing; "Joyful Reunion" treats an inspirational gathering, and "Goodbye to Melo" captures the sentiment experienced when leaving a familiar place and relates it to archetypal pilgrimage. *My Guitar* is within the same vein as the preceding two volumes to the degree that it treats the personal and the national within the prevailing *criollista* context.

Songs of the Payador Gabino Ezeiza contains versions of previously published poems, "The Guitar," "The Death of Moyano," "Fantasy," "Don Juan," and "The Volcano." Since Ezeiza was such a popular figure during this period, there was a fair amount of interest in having his works available in print, which inevitably led to some duplication. *Collection of the Songs of the Argentine Payador Gabino Ezeiza* consists of eleven selections. They are "Saludo al noble pueblo oriental" (Greetings to the noble Uruguayan people), "A los Treinta y Tres" (To be thirty-three), "La vida del payador" (The payador's life), "Un episodio del combate de San Lorenzo" (An episode from the Battle of San Lorenzo), "El remate" (The auction), "El cochero" (The coachman), "La visita" (The visit), "Doña Pascuala" (Doña Pascuala), "Amor platónico" (Platonic love), "Relación para cantar por cifra" (Tale to be told by numbers), and "Canto de contrapunto" (Contrapuntal song). As the titles suggest, these poems are dedicated to Uruguayans, the wars of independence, daily activities, and the trials and tribulations of the *payador.*

"The Payador's Life" is a tour de force of the errant bard's life. There is identification by the poet with the mythic *payador* who comes from a humble background, is orphaned, and then is condemned to a life of solitude:

> I was born of honorable parents,
> Although from a poor home,
> Living without any trouble
> Until I became aware.

I entered the age of dreams
Upon reaching fifteen years
When I felt disappointments
I already said: they are a lie!

Upon losing our mother
We suffered other pain;
We were left with a grandmother
Who died very old.
Our father at that time
Was fighting in Paraguay
And he was about to come home
When he also died.

(Nací de padres honrados,
Aunque de muy pobre cuna,
Pasando sin pena alguna
Hasta que tuve razón.
Entré en la edad de los sueños
Al llegar a los quince años,
Cuando sentí desengaños
Ya dije: ¡mentira son!

Al perder a nuestra madre
Otro dolor soportamos;
Con una abuela quedamos
Que de anciana falleció.
Nuestro padre en ese entonces
En el Paraguay luchaba
Y próximo a venir estaba
Cuando también falleció.)[21]

Orphanhood and solitude are two of the recurring themes in the poetry of the gaucho/payador. Sacrifice in the national interest is another thread common to the works of these three poets. In this poem, Ezeiza identifies with traditional commonplaces before finally personalizing this explication of his lifestyle:

21. Gabino Ezeiza, *Colección de canciones del payador argentino Gabino Ezeiza*, 13-14. Subsequent references will appear in the text as *GE*.

Sing Gabino, they tell me
I sing when they ask me to
But, people, never forget
That I have a heart.
Although you see my lips
Might etch a smile
Know that it is a calm breeze
After a strong north wind.

Yesterday the world saluted me
An Eden, a thousand springs.
And pleasant breezes
I felt kiss my face.
But then the deception
Dispelled the dense mystery,
I only find on this earth
Deceptions for me.

Because I spent my existence
Suffering bitterly,
Well there never existed in my mind
Happiness nor pleasure,
And only in my misfortune,
Pilgrim of life,
Each leaf which is detached
Will be run over on the ground.

I go about like a shipwrecked person, tied
To a pole which supports him,
Always hoping that the ship
Of salvation will come.
And when a cloud is seen
On the far off horizon
Says to another to expedite
Because another ship is coming.

Because I go, like a new Homer,
A beggar and wandering,
Singing everywhere
Where they give me shelter.

And in each of them
I say that I feel pain;
I go tied to a chain
Because my eagerness is sterile.

This is the truth, people,
Of all I have sung;
Remaining destroyed
In the flower of my youth.
At one time I have had
An illusory ambition
And when I have dreamed of glory
I found misery afterwards.

(Cante Gabino, me dicen;
Yo canto, cuando me piden,
Mas, señores, nunca olviden
Que yo tengo corazón.
Aunque vean que mis labios
Dibujan una sonrisa
Sepan que es cual mansa brisa
Después de fuerte aquilón.

El mundo ayer me brindaba
Un Eden, mil primaveras.
Y las auras placenteras
Besar mi frente sentí.
Mas luego que el desengaño
Descorrió su denso velo,
Tan solo encuentro en el suelo
Decepciones para mí.

Porque pasé mi existencia
Padeciendo amargamente,
Pues nunca existió en mi mente
Alegría ni placer,
Y solo en mi desventura,
Peregrino de la vida,
Cual hoja que desprendida
Se va en el suelo correr.

Voy como náufrago, asido
A un leño que le sostenga,
Siempre esperando que venga
La nave de salvación.
Y cuando ve alguna nube
En el lejano horizonte
Le dice a otro que se apronte,
Que viene una embarcación.

Porque voy, cual nuevo Homero,
Mendigo y peregrinando,
En todas partes cantando
Donde un asilo me dan.
Y así es que en todas ellas
Digo yo que siento pena;
Voy sujeto a una cadena,
Porque estéril es mi afán.

Esta es la verdad, señores,
De todo lo que he cantado;
Quedando yo aniquilado
En la flor de la niñez.
En un tiempo yo he tenido
Una ambición ilusoria
Y cuando he soñado gloria
Miseria encontré después.) (*GE,* 16–17)

For the poet, there is a built-in contradiction in the payador experience. On the one hand, there is the surface smile, followed by the deception inherent in the solitary vagabond life. There is the inevitable clash between expectations and the goals realized in life: "At one time I have had / An illusory ambition / And when I have dreamed of glory / I encountered misery afterwards." While payador life is perceived as romantic by many, there are some harsh realities played out on an individual level. But the suffering and disillusionment apparent in this poem is related to color as evidenced in family history as well as a perceived lack of societal respect.

In the introduction to *New Unpublished Songs of the Payador Gabino Ezeiza,* the editors praise the productivity and diversity of the poet: "That fertile imagination has produced so much that it would be difficult if not impossible to fit that torrent of improvisation into the reduced space of this book."[22] As it stands, the works of Ezeiza fill many volumes with a consistent emphasis upon *criollo* culture. Like the other volumes studied here, *New Songs* interprets the country and its inhabitants, but with more emphasis upon the role played by the various ethnic groups who compose the nation. "En la Plata" (In the River Plate region) is illustrative:

> Here the children live well
> from Poland and from France
> they excel through their arrogance
> All the children of Albion,
> here the Greek, the Austrian
> the Spaniard and Italian
> we call our brother
> blessed be that union.
>
> Blessed be this people
> who in such a manner rose up
> who had a blessed cause
> Which freed it,
> Which has not erased its origin
> being a cradle of brave ones
> and those who were slaves
> here gave them liberty.
>
> (Aquí viven bien los hijos
> de Polonia y de la Francia
> campean por su arrogancia
> todos los hijos de Albión,
> aquí el griego, el austriaco
> el español e italiano
> le llamamos nuestro hermano
> bendita sea esa unión.

22. Gabino Ezeiza, *Nuevas canciones inéditas del payador argentino Gabino Ezeiza,* 7. Subsequent references will appear in the text as *CI.*

> Bendito sea este pueblo
> que en tal forma se levanta
> que tuvo una causa santa
> la que lo independizó,
> que no ha borrado su origen
> siendo una cuna de bravos
> y los que fueron esclavos
> aquí libertad les dio.) (*CI*, 52–53)

As a nationalistic poet, Ezeiza gives credit to the various European components of the nation who were instrumental in cementing its social foundation. Perhaps he is a bit overzealous when treating the question of slavery and liberty, but nevertheless he follows the official line.

It is often assumed that Ezeiza lost his sense of identity as a black man in the criollization process, but the opposite becomes apparent in this volume of poetry. In the poem "Yo soy" (I am), the poet exclaims:

> I am of the race of Falucho
> which remains without inheritance
> spoke in a wheel
> which pulled a triumphant car;
> old shield that has saved
> the life of who carried it
> and with disdain threw it away
> when it became a hindrance.
>
> (Soy de la raza de Falucho
> que sin herencia se queda
> engranaje de una rueda
> que arrastró un carro triunfal;
> viejo escudo que ha salvado
> la vida a quien lo llevaba
> y con desdén lo arrojaba
> cuando le llegó a estorbar.) (*CI*, 42)

The black, a pariah, as the Other, is symbolized here as the poet uses the mythic Falucho as a cultural identity marker, then proceeds to criticize the practice of using Afro-Argentines to achieve, historically, objectives in war and then casting them aside. This motif recurs in much of Afro-Argentine discourse.

The most moving Afrocentric poem of Ezeiza, which is available in the volumes under scrutiny here, is "Un Oriental: ausente de su patria" (An Easterner: absent from his country). On first glance, the reader is tempted to think the poet is referring to nearby Uruguay because apparently he never traveled abroad, and because of the connotation of the noun "Oriental" (República Oriental del Uruguay). The images and metaphors, however, do not add up to such a reading:

> Far, very far away I find myself
> from that beloved homeland,
> whose memory my aching heart
> does not forget.
> Over there my eyes are fixed
> my hope is locked up over there
> where I adore the beautiful land
> where my mother was born.
>
> Oh homeland . . . I sigh for you
> and in a bitter broken cry
> I feel growing in my chest
> sadness and regret.
> From those beautiful fields
> filled for me with thorns,
> toward you I turn my eyes
> already tired of crying.
>
> Where do those valleys go
> and their beautiful shores
> on which gigantic palm trees
> show their elevation?
> Where are the beautiful mountains
> in which singing birds
> greet the dawns
> of the day as the sun is born?
>
> I would like to ease my sorrow,
> my pain and suffering;

I would like for one moment
to see your tropical sky.
But in my face destiny
has marked my luck
who could, homeland see you
for a moment no more.

Now I don't look at that arroyo
of fresh and crystalline water
that heads toward the Plata
with proved agitation.
I no longer listen to the songs
that the child then heard,
nor does happiness reign
in my poor heart.

I no longer look upon the village
where my cradle rocked me,
nor do I have the fortune
of admiring your blue sky.
I no longer look at the woodland
of that beautiful hot soil
nor the flourishing fertile plain
with which you saluted me,

I no longer admire that beautiful
clean and calm sky,
nor listen to the pleasant song
of the hummingbird on a flower.
And here I admire only
unfortunately, around me,
the fathomless emptiness
of my country and of my love.

From these faraway beaches
I want to see you, and it is in vain,
since the ocean is so large
as large as my grief.
Gather oh dear homeland!
my bitter and tiresome cry

as the memory of a son
who loves you from the heart.

(Lejos, muy lejos me encuentro
de aquella patria querida,
cuyo recuerdo no olvida
mi doliente corazón.
Allí están mis ojos fijos
mi esperanza allí se encierra
que adoro la hermosa tierra
donde mi madre nació.

Oh Patria . . . por ti suspiro
y en llanto amargo deshecho
siento crecer en mi pecho
la tristeza y el pesar.
Desde estos hermosos campos
llenos para mi de abrojos,
hacia ti vuelvo los ojos
ya cansados de llorar.

¿Dónde van aquellos valles
y sus hermosas riberas
en que gigantes palmeras
mostraban su elevación?
¿Dónde las lindas montañas
en que pájaros cantores
saludan los albores
del día al nacer el sol?

Quisiera templar mis penas,
mi dolor mi sufrimiento;
quisiera por un momento
ver tu cielo tropical.
Mas en mi frente el destino
tiene marcada la suerte
¡quién pudiera, patria verte
un minuto nada más!

Ya no miro aquel arroyo
de agua fresca y cristalina

que hacia el Plata se encamina
con soberbia agitación.
Ya no escucho los cantares
que entonces el niño oía,
ni reina va la alegría
en mi pobre corazón.

Ya no contemplo la aldea
donde me meció mi cuna,
ni tengo ya la fortuna
de admirar su cielo azul.
Ya no mireo las florestas
de aquel suelo hermoso ardiente
ni la vega floreciente
con que me brindabas tú,

Ya no admiro aquel hermoso
cielo límpido y sereno,
ni escucho el cantar ameno
del sum-sum sobre la flor.
Y aquí admiro solamente
por desgracia, en torno mío,
el insondable vacío
de mi patria y de mi amor.

Desde estas playas lejanas
quiero verte, y es en vano,
que es tan grande el océano
como grande es mi aflicción.
Recoje ¡oh patria querida!
mi llanto acerbo y prolijo
como el recuerdo de un hijo
que te ama de corazón.) (*CI*, 22–24)

Metaphors of distance, separation, and pain suggest both physical and psychological estrangement. The unnamed land where his mother was born evolves into virtually a paradise of beautiful rivers, mountains, palm trees, singing birds, and picturesque sunsets. Because of the physical and geographical images that are conjured up, this does not appear to be Uruguay or Argentina.

These verses convey a sense of loss, of alienation from an ethnic center that condemns the poet to perpetual exile in an uncaring world. The sense of estrangement is driven home in subsequent stanzas by "I no longer look/listen/contemplate." The poet is left with "the fathomless emptiness / of my homeland and my love." His final posture is one of rejection and longing. In spite of his acceptance as a black creole in Argentina, Gabino Ezeiza recognizes that something fundamental is missing.

Could the poet be referring to mythic paradisal Africa on a rhetorical level? The "ocean" he refers to is certainly not the La Plata estuary that separates Argentina and Uruguay. Instead, we have a search for roots, for a heritage that will help alleviate some of the pressures for blacks inherent in Argentine society. Therefore, Ezeiza expands the *criollo* metaphor to include the experiences of Afro-Argentines in the official culture. In conforming to the dictates of the national discourse, he mines the subsoil of Argentine popular culture, expresses himself in a style familiar to all, while at the same time maintaining a strong sense of his black personhood.

Like Horacio Mendizábal, Gabino Ezeiza is concerned with the representation of the Afro-Argentine as the Other. Afro-Argentines have been factored out of the national social equation and cast aside as estranged, alienated beings whose physical exile from Africa is permanent and who are constantly moving away from an ethnic center. This lack of an identity results in inner exile where marginalized people feel at odds with society, others, and themselves. The Afro-Argentine *payadores,* like their romantic counterparts, all "suffered the sentence of history— subjugation, domination, diaspora, displacement."[23] Their articulation of problems associated with "cultural difference, social authority and political discrimination" sustained a minority counterdiscourse that called into question many assumptions regarding Argentine cultural practices.

---

23. Homi K. Bhabha, "Postcolonial Criticism," in Stephen Greenblatt and Giles Gunn, eds., *Redrawing the Boundaries: The Transformation of English and American Literary Studies,* 437.

CONCLUSION
Cry for Afro-Argentines

In the inaugural issue of *El Proletario,* Lucas Fernández issued a warning that was not addressed seriously by the Afro-Argentine community. He stated: "The education of our brothers and sisters of color, will be, well one of our principal topics."[1] In its brief history (from April to June 1858), *El Proletario,* which could not sustain itself financially, addressed practical issues that were important to Afro-Argentines, such as education, unity, equality, discrimination, and demands in general, such as "reparation for the evils suffered for such a long time and our advancement and well-being and that of our children." At the same time, blacks were to take charge of their own destiny and not remain so dependent upon the majority culture.

These attitudes are echoed in a more impassioned way by Zenón Rolón in a controversial piece, "Dos palabras a mis hermanos de raza" (Two words to my brothers of the race), which was published twenty years later in *La Juventud:*

> Our race: to the present has lost the innocence of heart and the dignity of the individual: it spends life lazy, dissolute and depraved. The shout of freedom which resounded in its ear, it did not understand what it was, nor seized it with the honest happiness of those who aspire through it to work and learn; and not understanding that while it remained free of outside domination, it remained a slave to its base passions; and bad habits took the place of chains; and ignorance replaced vice.[2]

1. *El Proletario—Periódico Semanal, Politico, Literario y de Variedades* 1, no. 1 (18 de abril 1858): 1.
2. *La Juventud* 2d época, no. 20 (30 de junio 1878): 1.

Zenón's advice to his people is to work, learn a trade, become independent, educated—anything but a servant. His straightforward assessment of the problem with Afro-Argentines was met with charges of elitism and cultural superiority because of Zenón's status as a world-class composer. Needless to say, his call to arms fell upon deaf ears.

This lack of a common identity as a people and the inability to forge common goals has plagued Afro-Argentines from their arrival in Argentina to the present, as evidenced by the strife within organizations, the rivalry among competing newspapers, and the frustration of individual leaders.

There has not been an ongoing affirmation of Afro-Argentine culture to parallel the situation in Uruguay. Whereas across the La Plata estuary an organization such as the Asociación Cultural y Social Uruguay (ACSU) has existed for half a century, along with current socially responsible groups such as Mundo Afro, Afro-Argentine cultural activities have ceased. Although *Nuestra Raza,* the journal, has been defunct for years, the *Revista Bahía Hulan Jack* and *Mundo Afro* still strive to maintain an Afro-Uruguayan discourse.

The paucity of interest in Afro-Argentine matters was evident during the rare conference on Black Culture in the Americas, held in Buenos Aires in August 1991 and sponsored by the Instituto de Investigación y Difusión de las Culturas Negras Ilé Asé Osún Doyo, an Umbanda group composed of whites. Not only was there minimal attention devoted to the Afro-Argentine but also the protest against the lack of black participation and the constant treatment of the Afro-Argentine as *object* rather than as *subject* had to be spearheaded by the Mundo Afro group from Uruguay.

Two conference sessions in particular focused upon the black experience. "Historia, Aportes Culturales y Situación de la Comunidad Afro-Rioplatense en el Siglo XX" consisted of five papers. They were devoted to marriage practices among the Cape Verde population, Saint Baltasar's festival in Corrientes, the black image in Argentina at the beginning of this century, the black population of Santa Fe, and an account of Afro-Argentine family history from slavery to the present. "Historia y Aportes Culturales de los Afro-Rioplatenses hasta el Siglo XIX" contained four papers examining the black population in Buenos Aires, Catamarca, and Luján in past centuries. None of the presentations addressed the subject of Afro-Argentine literature. The most impressive presentation was by Tomás A. Platero, "Nuestra gran abuela María Clara: una historia de la esclavitud hacia la libertad," which reconstructed Platero family history from the sale of María Clara on the slave auction block in Montevideo in 1771 to the triumph of Tomás Braulio Platero as a scribe in 1902. A version of this search for African roots was published in the *Afro-Hispanic Review* in the spring of 1994.

The follow-up conference, Primer Congreso Internacional de Culturas Afro-Americanas, held September 7–11, 1993, again in Buenos Aires, did not represent an advancement over the first gathering. Again, the focus was primarily religious with very little attention devoted to Afro-Argentines. Papers included "Diversos aspectos relacionados con la esclavitud en el Río de la Plata, a través del estudio de Testamentos de Afro-Porteños 1750–1810," "Discurso Afro-Argentino: La reconstrucción de una tradición literaria," "Algunos ejemplos de la herencia africana en el ritmo," and "Cultos y ceremonias practicados por los africanos y sus descendientes en Buenos Aires entre los siglos XVIII y XIX." As two Argentine professors explained to me, investigations devoted to Afro-Argentines "are not in the national interest."

One individual who has devoted serious time and energy to investigating the Afro-Argentine experience is Tomás A. Platero, the author of *Lenguaje: cuaderno de poemas* (Language: notebook of poems, 1959), a slim volume of ten poems and *Lenguaje II: cuaderno de poemas* (Language II: notebook of poems, 1964), which also consists of ten selections. To my knowledge, this is the most recent publication of creative writing by an Argentine who acknowledges his African heritage. Platero, however, does not make ethnicity an essential component of his creative activity. The poems vary thematically and address patriotism, Buenos Aires, love, existence, life/death, religion, and loss. "Barca" (Ship) and "Poema de mi sed" (Poem of my thirst) are two of the best selections:

> Old structure upon remote waters
> renovated;
> ecstatic attitude;
> dying accent
> for a contest of profound absence of beings, of things;

days,
nights,
the hours and the stream chew on the hull of your life,
which is already dead.

There is neither cries nor crapes
only in turn
that vague nostalgia of oceans and ports visited

and a tear
of mine.

(Vieja arquitectura sobre remotas aguas
renovadas;
estática actitud;
acento moribundo
para un concurso de profundas ausencia de seres, de cosas,

días,
noches,
las horas y el riacho muerden el casco de tu vida,
que ya es muerte.

No hay llanto ni crespones;
sólo en torno,
esa vaga nostalgia de océanos y puertos recorridos,

y una lágrima
mía.)[3]

"Poem of My Thirst" is an expression of existential longing:

You wanted
only
to walk and more
the wide and high magnitude of my time.

Hardly if you wished
to take me from behind, surprised,

3. Tomás A. Platero, *Lenguaje: cuaderno de poemas*, 9.

and go over the time
of my hand

Now I wanted no more;
let me speak
and go over the touch of my hand
my reality, my past dreams

I wanted more than that:
to live,
make the past days
understand my voice.

And I wanted
afterwards, and never and always
to undertake the return of the voice
of my memory.

(Quería,
solamente,
andar y más
la magnitud ancha y alta de mi tiempo.

Apenas si quería
tomarme por la espalda, sorprendido,
y recorrer el tiempo
de mi mano.

Ya no quería más:
dejarme hablar,
y recorrer al dejo de la mano
mi realidad, mi sueño transcurridos.

Quería más que ésto:
vivir,
y hacer que los días transcurridos
entendieran mi voz.

Y quería,
después y nunca y siempre
emprender el retorno de la voz,
de mi memoria.) (21)

Platero's poetry is of absence, of longing, of trying to find a lost center, perhaps. "Ship" could very well be an ancestral allusion to the symbolic vehicle of the slave trade while "Poem of My Thirst" represents the desire to know more about that lost African identity.

Language II contains "Poema desde el vuelo" (Poem from flight), "Elegía del amor" (Elegy of love), "Poema de dios sin Dios" (Poem of god without God), "De la reconciliación con el poema" (About reconciliation with the poem), "Poema del campo de sangre" (Poem from the field of blood), "Poema de las letanías" (Poem of litanies), and "Las estaciones (Poema cíclico)" (The seasons [Cyclical poem])—"poema de la primera estación / segunda estación / tercera estación / cuarta estación" (Poem of the first / second / third / fourth season.) These selections continue the same esoteric focus as the previous volume. Platero, unlike the nineteenth-century Afro-Argentine writers, does not view ethnicity as the primary component of his poetics. Instead, he is concerned about the aesthetic value rather than the social value of poetry. *Language II* is concerned with "universal" themes such as love, the universe, the cyclical nature of existence, and solitude "About Reconciliation with the Poem" ends in the following manner:

> It changes the color of my skin
> because it is summer
> because I have freed myself from other clothes
> —and no one nor nothing can order that the
>   opposite happens with my skin
>   surrounded by its atmosphere
>   of this thing that I invest
>   and which is reality—
> to raise something more
> a new space
> animated
> where I
> and I
> will remain dialoguing for x time.
> Then
> I and I know through consecutive paradoxes
> that we have not lost everything
> that nothing belongs to us in absolute terms.

(Cambia el color de mi piel
porque es verano
porque me he liberado de otras ropas
—y nadie ni nada puede disponer que ocurra lo
   contrario con mi piel
   rodeada de su atmósfera
   de esta cosa que invento
   y que es realidad—
para levantar algo más
un nuevo espacio
animado
donde yo
y yo
permaneceremos dialogando por x tiempo.
Entonces
yo y yo sabemos por sucesivas paradojas
que no hemos perdido todo
que nada nos pertenece en términos de absoluto.)[4]

This poem is a meditation on being and nonbeing, on presence and absence, on the concrete and the illusory. In the final analysis, human existence is fragile at best, skin color a minor factor in the larger order of things.

In addition to the article published in the *Afro-Hispanic Review* and his poetry, Tomás A. Platero is in the process of creating an Asociación Socio-Cultural Afro-Argentina (Afro-Argentine Socio-Cultural Association). The goal of this organization is "To bring together the descendants of our black Africans, in an association—non-political, non-religious without profit motives—which would unravel, produce and support the testimonies of Afro-Argentine culture, praising and demonstrating its effective penetration, perpetuating it."[5]

The question of what happened to Afro-Argentines still intrigues the press. In a 1988 article in the *Atlanta Journal and Constitution* entitled

4. Tomás A. Platero, *Lenguaje II: cuaderno de poemas*, 26.
5. Tomás A. Platero, "Proyecto de creación de una Asociación Socio-Cultural Afro-Argentina" (1994).

"Buenos Aires Looks at Its 4,000 Blacks with Mixture of Curiosity and Prejudice," Matt Prichard writes

> Although they played important roles in Argentina's history, and although they accounted for nearly a third of the population of Buenos Aires at the start of the 19th century, blacks have become an object of curiosity and prejudice in what is often called 'the whitest city in Latin America.' Many Argentines believe the country's black population disappeared as a consequence of wars, disease and racial mixture. Another common belief is that along with the blacks, racism has disappeared from Argentina.[6]

Thus, the argument regarding the black presence in Argentina seems to have run full circle. It is evident that Afro-Argentines have played an important role in the development of that nation, but *what* concretely have they left to prove it? The answer to that question is at the core of this study. The fact that Afro-Argentines have not been perceived of as an integral component of the national ethos is due to the fact that they were unable to forge a collective identity and advocate for the common good. Aware of their precarious situation in a society that placed primarily negative emphasis upon blackness, they sought alternatives to perpetual otherness. Acculturation and miscegenation were the options most often pursued.

Finally, as efforts are continued to write blacks back into the literary history of Argentina and other Spanish American countries, there is a continuing tendency to disregard Afro-Hispanics. A case in point is *Between Civilization and Barbarism: Women, Nation, and Literary Culture in Modern Argentina* (1992) by Francine Masiello, which traces the presence of woman as object and subject in Argentine literature from romanticism to the current movement of the Mothers of the Plaza de Mayo. The words "Afro-Argentine" or "black" are not uttered once in the book, even when texts such as *El matadero, Amalia,* and other works of the Rosas era are discussed. Masiello's focus is

---

6. *The Atlanta Journal and Constitution,* September 4, 1988.

upon white women who, in the perception of Afro-Hispanics, were no different from their male counterparts.[7]

But Afro-Argentines refuse to disappear, and have combined internal black awareness with recurring stimuli from Uruguay. This is evident in the recent article "Rap del Candombe," which profiled the Uruguayan musical group "Bonga Martínez." In the article, Marta Dina gives a brief overview of the Afro-Argentine historical presence and concludes:

> The Africans who were uprooted from their lands and arrived here in the forced exile of slavery left a trail which remains and only wish that it is remembered and elevated to the place where it belongs: that of the authentic root of an identity which wished to be forgotten, as much by those who intended to achieve a white and European Argentina, where Africans and indigenous peoples did not have a place, as by those descendants who, fighting to better their life's conditions, were ashamed of their origin and wished to hide it. But the old lineages were not erased and are dispersed in families who don't know they possess them, not recognizing traits that appear time and again, throughout the generations.[8]

In spite of the tendency now to confuse Cape Verde blacks with descendants of the slave trade, Afro-Argentines remain alive and well in the national gene pool if not in the collective memory. Many primary texts documenting the Afro-Argentine presence no longer exist. Those available in the archives and libraries are in deplorable condition, due primarily to a lack of care and vandalism. But from the documents still available to us, it is possible to reconstruct some of the literary history of Afro-Argentines. Since writers usually reflect some of the tendencies of society, their message was that blacks were, except for a few, unable to overcome the social stigmas associated with slavery. Their choices were either to remain marginalized or to assimilate. Writers, too, had the same options: either write within mainstream conventions or remain voiceless for the majority. Given these choices, it is amazing that as much of an Afro-Argentine counterdiscourse emerged as in fact did.

---

7. Francine Masiello, *Between Civilization and Barbarism: Women, Nation, and Literary Culture in Modern Argentina*, 17–51.

8. Marta Diana, "Memoria: Rap del Candombe," 22.

Although the majority of Afro-Argentine written discourse has been lost, enough remains to allow us to draw important conclusions. Writers like Mendizábal, Thompson, Ezeiza, and others were aware of their past, present, and destiny in Argentina. Through their contributions and those of black journalists, a legacy of resistance to voicelessness is documented. While Afro-Argentine writers may never be accepted into the literary canon, some of them still speak to us through their works and in these pages.

BIBLIOGRAPHY

Books

Aguirre, Raúl Gustavo. *Antología de la poesía argentina*. 3 vols. Buenos Aires: Ediciones Librerías Fausto, 1979.

Anderson Imbert, Enrique. *Historia de la literatura argentina*. 2d ed., vol. 1. México: Fondo de Cultura Económica, 1970.

Andrews, George Reid. *Los afroargentinos de Buenos Aires*. Buenos Aires: Ediciones de la Flor, 1989.

———. *The Afro-Argentines of Buenos Aires: 1800-1900*. Madison. University of Wisconsin Press, 1980.

Arrieta, Rafael Alberto. *Historia de la literatura argentina*. Vol. 4. Buenos Aires: Ediciones Penser, 1959.

Ashcroft, Bill, Gareth Griffiths, and Helen Tiffin. *The Empire Writes Back: Theory and Practice of Post-Colonial Literature*. New York: Methuen, 1989.

Becco, Jorge Horacio. *El tema del negro en cantos, bailes, y villancicos de los siglos XVI y XVII*. Buenos Aires: Editorial Ollantay, 1951.

———. *Negros y morenos en el cancionero rioplatense*. Buenos Aires: Sociedad Argentina de Americanistas, 1953.

Benarós, León. *El desván de Clio: personajes, hechos, anécdotas y curiosidades de la historia argentina*. Buenos Aires: Editorial Fraterna, 1990.

Brathwaite, Edward Kamau. *Roots*. Ann Arbor: University of Michigan Press, 1993.

Castagnino, Raúl, ed. *Sociedades literarias argentinas*. La Plata: Facultad de Humanidades y Ciencia de la Educación, 1967.

Castillo, Tomás. *La Protectora, Sociedad de Socorros Mutuos: Memoria correspondiente al período administrativo 1912-1914*. Buenos Aires: E. L. Frigerio, 1914.

Chávez, Fermín. *La cultura en la época de Rosas: aportes a la descolonización mental de la Argentina*. Buenos Aires: Ediciones Theoria, 1973.

Colás, Santiago. *Postmodernity in Latin America: The Argentine Paradigm.* Durham: Duke University Press, 1994.

Coluccio, Felix. *Diccionario de voces y expresiones argentinas.* 2d ed. Buenos Aires: Editorial Plus Ultra, 1985.

Corominas, Joan. *Diccionario crítico etimológico de la lengua castellana.* 3 vols. Madrid: Gredos, 1954.

Cutolo, Vicente Osvaldo. *Nuevo diccionario biográfico argentino, 1750–1930.* Buenos Aires: Editorial Elche, 1985.

Davies, Carole Boyce. *Black Women, Writing and Identity: Migrations of the Subject.* New York: Routledge, 1994.

Elejalde, Santiago. *Consideraciones por un hombre del pueblo.* Buenos Aires: Imprenta de la Tribuna, 1880.

Endrek, Emiliano. *El mestizaje en Córdoba, siglos XVIII y principios del XIX.* Córdoba: Universidad Nacional de Córdoba, 1966.

Estrada, Marcos de. *Argentinos de origen africano.* Buenos Aires: Eudeba, 1979.

Fernández Moreno, César, and Horacio Jorge Becco. *Antología lineal de la poesía argentina.* Madrid: Editorial Gredos, 1968.

Finn, Julio. *Voices of Négritude.* New York: Quartet Books, 1988.

Ford, Jorge Miguel. *Beneméritos de mi estirpe.* La Plata: Tipografía de la Escuela de Artes y Oficios, 1899.

Foster, David William. *The Argentine Generation of 1880: Ideology and Cultural Texts.* Columbia: University of Missouri Press, 1990.

———. *Argentine Literature: A Research Guide.* 2d ed. New York: Garland, 1982.

Fuente, Alfredo de la. *El payador en la cultura nacional.* Buenos Aires: Ediciones Corregidor, 1986.

Gallardo, José Emilio. *Etnias africanas en el Río de la Plata.* Buenos Aires: Centro de Estudios Latinoamericanos, 1989.

Germani, Gino. *Política y sociedad en una época de transición: de la sociedad tradicional a la sociedad de masas.* 4th ed. Buenos Aires: Paidós, 1979.

Gesualdo, Vicente. *Historia de la música argentina.* 2 vols. Buenos Aires: Editorial Beta S. R. L., 1961.

Gobello, José. *Diccionario lunfardo.* 4th ed. Buenos Aires: Peña Lillo Editor, 1982.

Gorri, Gastón. *Inmigración y colonización en la Argentina.* 6th ed. Buenos Aires: Editorial Universitaria de Buenos Aires, 1988.

Graham, Richard, ed. *The Idea of Race in Latin America, 1870-1940.* Austin: University of Texas Press, 1990.

Greenblatt, Stephen, and Giles Gunn, eds. *Redrawing the Boundaries: The Transformation of English and American Literary Studies.* New York: Modern Language Association of America, 1992.

Ingenieros, José. *La locura en la Argentina.* Buenos Aires: Editorial Tor, 1955.

Jackson, Richard L. *Black Writers in Latin America.* Albuquerque: University of New Mexico Press, 1979.

JanMohamed, Abdul R., and David Lloyd, eds. *The Nature and Context of Minority Discourse.* New York: Oxford University Press, 1990.

Kadir, Djelal. *The Other Writing: Postcolonial Essays in Latin America's Writing Culture.* West Lafayette: Purdue University Press, 1993.

Kordón, Bernardo. *Candombe: contribución al estudio de la raza negra en el Río de la Plata.* Buenos Aires: Editorial Continente, 1938.

Lago, Catalina E. *Buenos Aires, 1858: Panorama artístico de la ciudad a través de sus diarios.* Buenos Aires: Universidad de Buenos Aires, 1961.

Lahourcade, Alicia Nydia. *La comunidad negra de Chascomús y su reliquia.* Chascomús: Talleres Gráficos Chacabuco, 1973.

Lanuza, José Luis, ed. *Los morenos.* Buenos Aires: Emecé, 1942.

————. *Morenada.* Buenos Aires: Emecé, 1946.

————. *Morenada: una historia de la raza africana en el Río de la Plata.* Buenos Aires: Editorial Schapire, 1967.

Lara, Tomás de, Inés Leonilda, and Ronetti de Panti. *El tema del tango en la literatura argentina.* 2d ed. Buenos Aires: Ediciones Culturales Argentinas, 1968.

Leitch, Vincent B. *Cultural Criticism, Literary Theory, Poststructuralism.* New York: Columbia University Press, 1992.

Ludmer, Josefina. *El género gauchesco: un tratado sobre la patria.* Buenos Aires: Editorial Sudamericana, 1988.

Mafud, Julio. *Psicología de la viveza criolla.* 7th ed. Buenos Aires: Distal S. R. L., 1988.

Masiello, Francine. *Between Civilization and Barbarism: Women, Nation, and Literary Culture in Modern Argentina.* Lincoln: University of Nebraska Press, 1992.

Masini, José Luis. *La esclavitud en Mendoza: época independiente.* Mendoza: Talleres Gráficos D'Accurzio, 1962.

Mendizábal, Ernesto. *Domingo F. Sarmiento.* Buenos Aires: Penser, 1895.

————. *Hectór F. Varela: su semblanza*. Buenos Aires: Jacobo Penser, 1887.

Molinari, Diego Luis. *La trata de negros: datos para su estudio en el Río de la Plata*. 2d ed. Buenos Aires: Universidad de Buenos Aires, 1944.

Moya, Ismael. *El arte de los payadores*. Buenos Aires: Editorial P. Berruti, 1959.

Natale, Oscar. *Buenos Aires, negros y tango*. Buenos Aires: Peña Lillo Editor, 1984.

Onega, Gladys S. *La inmigración en la literatura argentina (1880-1910)*. Buenos Aires: Centro Editor, 1982.

Ortiz Oderigo, Nestor R. *Aspectos de la cultura africana en el Río de la Plata*. Buenos Aires: Editorial Plus Ultra, 1974.

————. *Calunga: Croquis del Candombe*. Buenos Aires: Eudeba, 1969.

————. *Rostros de bronce: músicos negros de ayer y de hoy*. Buenos Aires: Mirasol, 1964.

Pampín, Manuel. *La historia del tango: sus orígenes*. Buenos Aires: Ediciones Corregidor, 1976.

Pereda Valdés, Ildefonso. *Antología de la poesía negra americana*. 2d ed. Montevideo: BUDA, 1953.

————. *El negro rioplatense y otros ensayos*. Montevideo: Claudio García, 1937.

Prieto, Adolfo. *El discurso criollista en la formación de la Argentina moderna*. Buenos Aires: Editorial Sudamericana, 1988.

Puccia, Enrique H. *Breve historia del carnaval porteño*. Buenos Aires: Municipalidad de la Ciudad de Buenos Aires, 1974.

Quereilhac de Kussrow, Alicia G. *La fiesta de san Baltasar: presencia de la cultura negra en el Plata*. Buenos Aires: Ediciones Culturales Argentinas, 1980.

Quinteros, Mamerto Fidel. *Memorias de un negro del congreso*. Buenos Aires: L. J. Rosso y Cia, 1924.

Ramallo, Jorge María. *Historia Argentina fundamental*. Buenos Aires: Ediciones Braga, 1987.

Ríos, José. *Cayetano silva*. Montevideo: Mi Artículo, 1973.

Rodríguez Molas, Ricardo. *La música y danza de los negros en el Buenos Aires de los siglos XVIII y XIX*. Buenos Aires: Ediciones CLIO, 1957.

————. *La primitiva poesía gauchesca anterior a Bartolomé Hidalgo*. Buenos Aires: Talleres Gráficos Lumen, 1958.

————. *Luis Pérez y la biografía de Rosas escrita en verso en 1830*. Buenos Aires: CLIO, 1957.

Rojas, Ricardo. *Historia de la literatura argentina: los modernos.* Buenos Aires: Editorial Guillermo Craft, 1957.

Román, Marcelino M. *Itinerario del payador.* Buenos Aires: Editorial Lautaro, 1957.

Romay, Francisco L. *El barrio de Monserrat.* 3d ed. Buenos Aires: Municipalidad de la Ciudad de Buenos Aires, 1971.

————. *Historia de Chascomús.* Chascomús: Centro de Publicaciones Municipales, 1967.

Rossi, Vicente. *Cosas de negros.* 2d ed. Buenos Aires: Hachette, 1958.

Rudione, Alfredo V. E., ed. *En torno al criollismo.* Buenos Aires: Centro Editor de América Latina, 1983.

Sánchez Sivori, Amalia. *Diccionario de payadores.* Buenos Aires: Plus Ultra, 1979.

Santiago, José Alberto. *Antología de la poesía argentina.* Madrid: Editora Nacional, 1973.

Santo, Víctor di. *El canto del payador en el circo criollo.* Buenos Aires: Talleres Gráficos Offset 25, 1987.

Scenna, Miguel Angel. *Cuando murió Buenos Aires.* Buenos Aires: Ediciones La Bastilla, 1974.

Seibel, Beatriz. *El cantar del payador: antología.* Buenos Aires: Ediciones del Sol, 1988.

Senet, Honorio J. *De lo nuestro.* La Plata: Talleres Gráficos Olivieri y Domínguez, 1927.

Soler Cañas, Luis. *Negros, gauchos y compadres en el cancionero de la Federación (1830-1848).* Buenos Aires: Ediciones Theoría, 1958.

————. *Orígenes de la literatura lunfarda.* Buenos Aires: Ediciones Siglo Veinte, 1965.

Studer, Elena F. S. de. *La trata de negros en el Río de la Plata durante el siglo XVII.* Buenos Aires: Universidad de Buenos Aires, 1958.

Thorpe, James, ed. *The Aims and Methods of Scholarship in Modern Languages and Literatures.* New York: Modern Language Association of America, 1963.

Wilde, José Antonio. *Buenos Aires desde setenta años atrás (1810-1880).* 6th ed. Buenos Aires: Editorial Universitaria de Buenos Aires, 1977.

Periodicals

Aguirre, Máximo. "El destino color de piel." *La Prensa: Secciones Ilustradas de los Domingos* (9 de enero 1972): 5.

Anon. "Buenos Aires de Ebano." *Revista Clarín* (5 de diciembre 1971): 34-39.

Anon. "Recordando el pasado." *Caras y Caretas* (mayo 1927): unpaginated.

Anon. "Relación de las sociedades de morenos africanos establecidas con permiso de la autoridad, con expresión de sus fondos, cuarteles y calles en que existen, y el tiempo en que fueron autorizadas." *Crónica política y literaria de Buenos Aires* 24 (3 de mayo 1827): 2.

Avellaneda, Andrés. "Calendario—Mayo de 1812: prohibe la junta el ingreso de esclavos." *La Opinión* (28 de mayo 1976): 8.

Benarós, León. "Negros en Buenos Aires." *Todo es historia* 40 (agosto 1970): 24-25.

Blomberg, Hector Pedro. "Gabino Ezeiza, el último payador." *Aquí Está* 8, no. 793 (23 de diciembre 1943): 8-11.

———. "Los negros de Buenos Aires." *Aquí Está* 14, no. 1340 (21 abril 1949): 18-19, 23.

Boj, Silverio. "La poesía negra en Indoamérica." *Sustancia: Revista de Cultura Superior* 1 (marzo 1940): 591-608.

Bonet, Carmelo M. "El argentino de ayer, de hoy y de mañana." *Buenos Aires—Revista de Humanidades* 1, no. 1 (1961): 99-126.

Bosch, Mariano G. "Gabino Ezeiza: sepelio de los restos." *La Prensa* (14 de octubre 1916): 7.

———. "Los negros de los abuelos." *Aquí Está* 6, no. 541 (24 de julio 1941): 4-5, 25.

Castro, Donald S. "El negro del acordeón: The Image of the Black in Argentina." *Afro-Hispanic Review* (January, May, September 1988): 11-18.

Colás, Santiago. "Of Creole Symptoms, Cuban Fantasies, and Other Latin American Postcolonial Ideologies." *PMLA* 110, no. 3 (May 1995): 382-96.

Deleuze, Gilles, and Félix Guattari. "What is a Minor Literature?" *Mississippi Review* 11, no. 3 (1983): 18.

Diana, Marta. "Memoria: Rap del Candombe." *Clarín,* 1 de noviembre 1992, 22.

Figarillo. "El carnaval antiguo: los candomberos." *Caras y Caretas* 4, no. 175 (8 de febrero 1902): n.p.

Fontanella de Weinberg, María Beatriz. "Variedades lingüísticas usadas por la población negra rioplatense." *Boletín de la Academia Argentina de Letras* 51, nos. 201-2 (1986): 283-86.

Frigerio, Alejandro. "El candombe argentino: crónica de una muerte anunciada." *Revista de Investigaciones Folklóricas* 8 (diciembre 1993): 50-60.

———. "La Umbanda no es una religión de ignorantes y mediocres." *Revista de Antropología* 6, no. 10 (1991): 22-33.

Gálvez, Victor. "La raza africana en Buenos Aires." *Nueva Revista de Buenos Aires* 3, no. 8 (1883): 246-60.

García Barrios, Constance. "The Black in Literature about the Rosas Era." *Revista/Review Interamericana* 10, no. 4 (winter 1980/1981): 476-87.

Garganigo, John F. "El perfil del negro en la narrativa rioplatense." *Historiografía y Bibliografía Americanistas* 21 (1977): 71-109.

Gesualdo, Vicente. "Los negros en Buenos Aires y el interior." *Historia* 2, no. 5 (marzo-mayo 1982): 26-49.

Goldberg, Marta B. "La población negra y mulata de la ciudad de Buenos Aires, 1810-1840." *Desarrollo Económico* 16, no. 61 (abril-julio 1976): 75-99.

Hutcheon, Linda. "Colonialism and the Postcolonial Condition: Complexities Abounding." *PMLA* 110, no. 1 (January 1995): 7-16.

Kubayanda, Josaphat Bekunuru. "Minority Discourse and the African Collective: Some Examples from Latin American and Caribbean Literature." *Cultural Critique* 6 (spring 1987): 113-30.

Laguarda Trias, Rolando A. "Afronegrismos rioplatenses." *Boletín de la Real Academia Española* (enero-abril 1969): 27-116.

Matamoro, Blas. "Los negros han desaparecido del ámbito de Buenos Aires (tras siglos de guerra, esclavitud, candombes y tango)." *La Opinión* (6 de julio 1976): 17.

McMillen, Liz. "Post-Colonial Studies Plumb the Experience of Living Under, and After, Imperialism." *Chronicle of Higher Education,* May 19, 1993, A6-9.

Miguez, Eduardo José. Revision of *The Afro-Argentines of Buenos Aires, 1800-1900* in *Anuario Instituto de Historias Sociales.* Universidad Nacional del Centro de la Provincia de Buenos Aires, no. 3 (1988): 407-10.

"Nuestros negros." *Todo es historia* 162 (noviembre 1980): Número especial.

Olgo Ochoa, Pedro. "El invento de Falucho." *Todo es historia* 41 (septiembre 1970): 33-39.

Ortiz de Marco, Enrique. "El negro en la formación étnica y sociocultural argentina." *Boletín del Centro Naval* 680 (julio–septiembre 1969): 363–81.

Ortiz Oderigo, Nestor. "Gabino Ezeiza: para una historia con payadores." *El Mundo* (10 de octubre 1965): 46.

———. "La influencia africana en el castellano del Río de la Plata." In José Joaquín Montes, ed. *Estudios sobre español de América y lingüística afroamericana* (Bogotá: Instituto Caro y Cuervo, 1989): 280–88.

Patti, Pedro. "Una morena asoma en el teatro porteño." *Aquí Está* 11, no. 1064 (29 de julio 1946): 8–9.

Platero, Tomás. "Nuestra gran abuela María Clara: una historia de la esclavitud hacia la libertad." *Afro-Hispanic Review* 13, no. 1 (spring 1994): 52–54.

Posadas, Manuel T. "Las poesías del joven Thompson." *La Juventud* 18 (10 de junio 1878): 1–2.

Prichard, Matt. "Buenos Aires Looks at Its 4,000 Blacks with Mixture of Curiosity and Prejudice." *Atlanta Journal and Constitution,* September 4, 1988.

"Relación de los Presidentes y Socios que pertenecen a las sociedades africanas." *La Gaceta Mercantil: Diario Comercial, Político y Literario* (25 de junio 1842): 2.

Rodríguez Molas, Ricardo. "Condición social de los últimos descendientes de los esclavos rioplatenses (1852–1900)." *Cuadernos Americanos* 3 (mayo–junio 1962): 133–70.

———. "El negro en el Río de la Plata." *Historia Integral Argentina* 1 (1974): 38–56.

———. "El negro en la sociedad porteña después de Caseros." *Comentario* 6, no. 22 (1959): 45–55.

———. "El primer libro de entrada de esclavos negros a Buenos Aires." *Revista de la Universidad* (La Plata), no. 2 (octubre–diciembre 1957): 139–43.

———. "Esclavitud africana, religión y origen étnico." *Ibero-Amerikanisches Archiv,* N.F. Jg 14 H. 2 (1988): 125–47.

———. "Horacio Mendizábal: poeta de color en el Buenos Aires del siglo XIX." *Universidad* (Santa Fe), no. 37 (enero–junio 1958): 159–69.

———. "Negros libres rioplatenses." *Buenos Aires—Revista de Humanidades* 1, no. 1 (1961): 99–126.

Saenz Quesada, María. "Los negros en nuestro país: La lenta integración de una raza transplantada." *Clarín: Cultura y nación* (2 de noviembre 1978): 1–3.

Senet, Rodolfo. "¿Cómo improvisaba Gabino?" *La Prensa* 2d sec. (24 de junio 1928): 5.

Simpson, Máximo. "Porteños de color." *Panorama* 49 (junio 1967): 78–85.

Soiza Reilly, Juan José. "Gente de color." *Caras y Caretas* 8, no. 373 (25 de noviembre 1905): n.p.

Soler Cañas, Luis. "Gabino Ezeiza en el cancionero popular cuyano," *Clarín* 2d sec. (7 de octubre 1956): 8.

———. "Gabino Ezeiza: verdad y leyenda." *Todo es historia* 1, no. 2 (1967): 65–77.

———. "Pardos y morenos en el año 80 . . ." *Revista del Instituto de Investigaciones Juan Manuel de Rosas* 23 (enero-diciembre 1963): 272–309.

Thompson, Era Bell. "Argentina: Land of the Vanishing Blacks." *Ebony* 28, no. 12 (October 1973): 74–85.

Torre Revello, José. "El último payador: Gabino Ezeiza." *La Razón* (13 de octubre 1916): 6.

———. "Noticia de algunos artistas coloniales." *Síntesis* 2, no. 18 (noviembre 1928): 333–44.

Ulanovsky Sack, Daniel. "Los argentinos que no tienen derecho a mostrarse." *Clarín* (14 de febrero 1993): 16.

Zamudio Silva, Jorge. "Para un caracterización de la sociedad del Río de la Plata (siglos XVI a XVIII): la contribución africana." *Revista de la Universidad de Buenos Aires* tercera época 3, no. 2 (abril-junio 1945): 293–314.

Authors

Cazón, Higinio. *Alegrías y pesares: canciones nacionales.* Buenos Aires: Maucci, n.d.

Ezeiza, Gabino. *Canciones del payador argentino Gabino Ezeiza: nueva y última colección.* Buenos Aires: Luis Maucci y Cia., 1892.

———. *Canciones del payador Gabino Ezeiza.* 2d ser. Montevideo: Librería Argentina, 1885.

———. *Canciones del payador Gabino Ezeiza, primera parte.* Buenos Aires: Luis Maucci y Cia., 1896.

————. *Cantares criollos por Gabino Ezeiza, payador argentino.* Buenos Aires: N. Tommasi, 1886.

————. *Colección de canciones del payador argentino Gabino Ezeiza.* Montevideo: Casa Editora Calle de Andes, 1897.

————. *Contrapunto entre los payadores Gabino Ezeiza y Pablo Vázquez.* Rosario de Santa Fe: Alfonso Longo, n.d.

————. *Mi guitarra: versos alegres, cuentos, historias, etc.* Buenos Aires: Luis Maucci y Cia., 1895.

————. *Nuevas canciones inéditas del payador argentino Gabino Ezeiza.* Buenos Aires: Biblioteca Gauchesca, 1897.

————. *Recuerdos del payador.* Buenos Aires: Andrés Pérez Cuberes, 1946.

García, Luis. *Gauchesco.* Buenos Aires: La Minerva Tandil, n.d.

————. *Esquinas líricas: versos.* Buenos Aires: Talleres Gráficos L. López, 1937.

Mendizábal, Horacio. *Himnos sagrados.* Buenos Aires: Sociedad Americana de Tratados, 1870.

————. *Horas de meditación.* Buenos Aires: Imprenta de Buenos Aires, 1869.

————. *Primeros versos.* Buenos Aires: Imprenta de Buenos Aires, 1865.

Platero, Tomás. *Lenguaje I: cuaderno de poemas.* La Plata: Municipalidad de la Plata, 1959.

————. *Lenguaje II: cuaderno de poemas.* La Plata: Fondo Nacional de las Artes, 1964.

INDEX